TEACH US TO PRAY

Learning a Little About God

ANDRÉ LOUF

TEACH US TO PRAY

Learning a Little About God

Translated by Hubert Hoskins

PAULIST PRESS
New York/Ramsey/Toronto

A Deus Books Edition of Paulist Press, © 1974 Darton, Longman and Todd Ltd., originally published as *Heer, Leer Ons Bidden* by Editions Lannoo Tielt, Belgium.

U.S. Edition copyright ©1975 Franciscan Herald Press, Chicago, Ill.

Library of Congress
Catalog Card Number: 76-49322

ISBN: 0-8091-2001-1

Published by Paulist Press
Editorial Office: 1865 Broadway, N.Y., N.Y. 10023
Business Office: 545 Island Road, Ramsey, N.J. 07446

Printed and bound in the
United States of America

CONTENTS

5

FOR FATHER AND MOTHER
WHOM I FREQUENTLY SAW AT PRAYER
AND FROM WHOM I LEARNED TO PRAY

FOR MY FATHERS AND BROTHERS
IN JESUS CHRIST
WHO HAVE SHOWN ME THE WAY TO MY HEART

INTRODUCTION

The purpose of this short book is to do just a little to appease the hunger for prayer; a hunger to be found here, there and everywhere in these days. Of theological studies about prayer—and very good ones at that—there are already enough. A personal testimony is much more difficult to come out with, not only because it involves oneself—and nobody likes beating his own drum—but also because prayer emanates from a particular zone within a person. This inmost recess is not much talked about, and most of us have not so far ventured down into it.

Of course, we know so very little about ourselves; very little about our bodies and a lot less, even, about the invisible life going on inside us. We are accustomed to living on the outer edge of our selves, on the surface, never under the skin, while deep down inside us there is an area neglected and ignored because we have no inkling of its existence.

Jesus said of the celibate state that not everyone can attain to it, but only those to whom it has been given (Matt. 19:11). This is true also of prayer. No one can get a grasp of it unless it is given him so to do. It is not there just for the taking. You can't master it by force; nor can you put it up for sale. How could you convey the taste of a mango to someone who has never tried it?

Speaking about prayer can only mean 'bearing witness to it'. A testimony proves nothing, refutes nothing, is not persuasive. It either strikes home or it does not. In other words, a piece of testimony will only mean something to another person if it finds in him a responsive echo, and releases in him something that strikes an answering chord.

This little book is intended to be a testimony to prayer. It has been the author's privilege to listen, not infrequently, to people of the past and of the present at prayer. He has tried to penetrate to the very core of their experience, has tried to put it into simple and up-to-date language. He may sometimes give the impression of talking about prayer in a novel and surprising way. In fact he is constantly having recourse to material which is part and parcel of a long tradition, and extends far back into the early history of spirituality. So the familiar vocabulary of prayer in more recent centuries will not be much in evidence here. On the contrary we shall be drawing liberally on the ancient monastic writers. After all, the author is himself a monk. It is in daily contact with the Bible, the Word of God, with the writings of the Fathers and of earlier monks, that the monk leads his life of contemplation and prayer. He works, sleeps and eats like everyone else; but all that he does is centred on prayer. That is why he has adopted a life of solitude and quietness. He attempts in a plain and simple fashion to look after his own livelihood and meet his needs. The free time thus made available he spends in prayer, searching unceasingly after the face of God.

This is his only recreation. And also his main task. For the monk knows from experience that only in that exercise, in prayer, will he be fully himself: a man-for-people and a man-for-God. That too in the other sense of these two phrases: man-on-behalf-of-the-people and man-before-the-face-of-God.

Every person disposed to do so can heed this testimony. For within himself he contains a soil nourishing enough for the Word to germinate and bear fruit in it. Only he must not allow the thistles to choke it, nor the sun's heat to burn it up. For whoever tends and nurtures the Word, for him it will bear its fruit, thirty-, sixty-, a hundredfold. And the fruit will last to eternity.

Oral prayer is in rather a poor way nowadays, if it has not actually fallen into discredit. On the other hand there is a good deal of interest, no doubt often crude and uninformed, in the interior life of the individual, where prayer is thought to be located. Hence the ever-growing concern with all sorts of techniques, psychological and physical, of recollection and meditation. The writing of this book has entailed keeping these modern aspects of the search for prayer constantly in mind. It is an attempt to explain to the contemporary reader in vernacular terms how the time-honoured instructors and masters of prayer had already found an answer to these questions. With them, techniques of prayer, verbal prayer and interior prayer together run into a harmonious whole in which the Holy Spirit is continuously at work within us.

A few of the articles I published earlier on have been used here again, in part and in a revised form. I wish therefore to thank the editors of the journals in question for their permission to republish.

The free time I needed in order to complete this book my confrères gladly and graciously allowed to me; and because that time was also theirs, I must acknowledge my gratitude and indebtedness to them for it.

PRAYING—IS IT ON NOWADAYS?

We know so very little about praying. It is a mystery which, we suspect, must lie secluded somewhere deep in the recesses of the heart. Like other mysteries of human life: the birth of a new being, the love that burgeons and comes to flower, the ordeal that has its climax in death, and what follows upon death. All this evokes mixed feelings in a man. Longing alternates with fear, and love with awe. Until these values are turned into a personal value, unless they have been assimilated and so become a personal acquisition, the individual remains a self divided. He feels, simultaneously, impulse and counter-impulse. He is attracted and he is repelled.

It always has been difficult, of course, to write about prayer—more so today than ever before. Until a man has accepted prayer as the mysterious and yet deepest centre of his being, it must always be hard for him to utter on the subject. He may enthuse; but his words will have a spurious and hollow ring. Or he may speak critically, even mordantly, of prayer; but the very vehemence of his reaction will betray the hidden need, aching like an incurable wound inside him.

That dialectic is a typical mark of the Church in our time. If some are abandoning prayer, as many others are seeking to enquire and learn about it. This situation is an inevitable and even a healthy one. It means, primarily, two things: first, that we still lack the ability to pray. Second, that at long last we are aware of the fact.

One of the Fathers—a monk of the very early period—confronted his pupils with a hard question which they all attempted to answer. When it came to the turn of the last one to speak, he said: 'I don't know'. The monk commended him for it. He had made the right answer.[1]

We try so often, do we not, to find an easy solution to the questions with which life is continually confronting us. To save face or quieten conscience we come up with something or other—but it is not the *right* answer at all. We are satisfied too quickly. The disciple of that old monk spoke the truth: he did not know and was humble enough to admit his ignorance. The proper response was lowly awe in face of the mystery. So too for us: the first and most fundamental truth about prayer is to know that we are unable to pray. 'Lord, teach us how to pray' (Luke 11:1).

Crisis

In time past—and not so very long ago at that—this was not so obvious. We used to feel a certain assurance. In the Church as well. The Church's structures formed a solid edifice. There was nothing ambiguous about the rules and injunctions. Sometimes we felt we were well rid of the need to do our own thinking. The thinking was done for us. But in recent years we have seen a definite process of evolution in our society. Even the Church has been due for a face-lift. The second Vatican Council set people's minds in a whirl. Aggiornamento, experimentation, renewal, the words have a familiar ring to every ear. Instead of living out their Christianity in strictly personal terms, people now are looking for ways of giving more prominence to the communal aspect. Helping one's neighbour—the fact of our common humanity—is the centre of attention. And prayer—what purpose does that serve? And can we still pray?

People have always wondered about prayer; and invariably, when they thought they had the answer, it has turned out to be inadequate. The main question used to be: 'What is prayer?' But now, all of a sudden, we no longer know *whether* we are still praying. We used to know that, at least. There was no doubt about praying, as such. Prayer was then one practice, one exercise, among the rest, prescribed and sometimes dished up according to rule, like other spiritual exercises. There were prayer-methods in plenty. People tried to be faithful, often with real openheartedness, to what was called with more or less emphasis on the possessive pronoun *their* meditation. And they would talk about prayer *succeeding* or, conversely, *being a failure*. Whatever it turned out to be—it must surely, on occasion, have been authentic prayer—the vocabulary of prayer at that time had a very triumphalist complexion. Prayer appeared to be an exercise in which, besides grace, a lot of human ingenuity and resource were called for.

But nowadays everything has suddenly become quite different: no longer are we able to say whether we are still engaged in prayer or even whether we still believe in the possibility of prayer. In the old days prayer may have been far too easy; now it has all of a sudden become unspeakably difficult. Was it prayer at all, then? And how or where are we to pray now?

Was it in fact prayer? Most of us do not know what to reply to such a question. The set phrases, methods, instructions (including the rubrics attached to every conceivable form of prayer) that were in vogue some thirty years ago have fallen into disuse, are ignored or at any rate have been fundamentally altered, in certain cases completely replaced, even, by something else. Prayers are no longer

12

reeled off. There is a prevailing attitude of distrust towards set prayers 'tacked on from outside' and towards the formalism they may engender. But people have come to be equally afraid of *interior* prayer, so called; and most of them no longer have any time for it. Those who do find the time are for the most part unable to achieve an interior peace and quiet.

As a taciturn and withdrawn temperament might be supposed to assist the process of acquiring and maintaining such tranquillity, the question still arises—tinged indeed with suspicion and sometimes with irony—as to what is in fact achieved by the resolve to pray. The cold walls of our own total seclusion? The storms that rage within a frustrated mind and heart? The unattainable object of wants and desires, projected into infinitude, yes, and into heaven itself? A meagre consolation for having lost the courage to endure and cope with the sober realities of everyday life as an ordinary average human being? A cheap gesture of resignation because everything and everybody lay too heavy a charge upon us? Is prayer, then, a flight into unreality, into dream, illusion, romanticism? The truth is, we are at our wits' end. We have lost the scent of prayer altogether. We are caught in the blind alley of an illusion. Many of us have touched zero-point.

Thank God! For now we can make a new start. That zero-point can mean a reversal, a turn of the tide. For this is the saving grace of our time, in the Church of today: that we are now at our wits' end. That the props have suddenly collapsed. That now at last we can see how little of the façade remains or indeed was ever there at all. And that now the Lord can build everything up again, from scratch. There has come down to us from one of the early Fathers of the Church a profound saying: 'Prayer is as yet imperfect where the monk continues to be conscious of it and knows that he is at prayer.'[2] One thing is sure: few venture to think they have this knowledge. And that in itself is a sign of grace.

The hunger for prayer

Here then, is the paradox of a crisis which could yet prove to be a fruitful one. Although the practice of prayer in its various forms may be in decline, never was the hunger for prayer greater than it is now, more especially among the young.

The great cultural changes we are living through today have sparked off something in many people. But what? For the most part they do not even know themselves. They feel an impulse, a hunger for an inner experience. It is a driving force within them. They cannot just dig in and do nothing. They have to make some discovery. But of what? Could drugs be the answer? A freer approach to sex—will that liberate them? They are giving it a try; but the sheer monotony of it soon serves to demonstrate how hollow all this

13

is. It is like the fate of the mayfly, who briefly glimpses the daylight and then dies. But the hunger persists—an unsatisfied and ever more insistent hunger.

It is the youngsters in particular who feel this. Often enough, their way of expressing this impulse, this drive, is to take themselves off to foreign parts. We can no longer provide them with the answer. At any rate, that is what they think. One comes across them here, there and everywhere; and they are often easy to recognize. They go off to Taizé, pitch their tent, join with the brothers quite spontaneously in prayer and open up their feelings and experiences to one another. For an experience, that they will have. And to find it they will put a great deal behind them, will journey on from one experience to another. Forgetting what is behind, they press on ... and on.

Here and there in this world some corners are left where prayer fills the whole atmosphere, as it were. There are still some people for whom praying is like drawing breath. Anyone who has toiled under the blazing sun of Mt. Athos will never be able to forget the praying monks whom he is bound to have met there, their faces aflame and their glance like fire: penetrating, yet so infinitely gentle and utterly tender. Men who out of the profoundest depths of the self, are outgoing towards everything and everybody, who are able to discover the inner fire in people and things—the 'hidden heart of things' (Isaac the Syrian)—who expose their deepest core in measureless love and understanding.

Besides the solitaries who pray, you can also find groups who pray together. In Russia and Romania the night offices are crowded, the churches packed still today with young and old together.

The hunger for prayer sometimes sends these seekers out to the Far East. At this very moment hundreds of young people from the West are staying in the *ashrams* of India and Japan, with the idea of being initiated and directed by a *guru* in the techniques of meditation. In the western hemisphere too, techniques such as Zen and Yoga are claiming much attention. People will go to any trouble or expense to achieve control of mind and body. They want to be free, to free themselves to be the recipients of spiritual experience. These techniques are really a form of *ascesis*, the purpose of which is to direct a person's attention away from what is superficial and unrewarding in order to concentrate it on the very heart of things. First and foremost, on the innermost, essential core of the person himself. He has to attain a degree of harmony with his deepest 'I' and at the same time with other human beings and with the world as a whole. Finally, with God as well. That is, at any rate for the believer. This experience is a genuine process of self-realization. It is fairly unusual and is best likened to a rebirth. In Zen it is known as *illumination*. The experience also confers a certain interior contemplative vision in consequence of which everything else is seen from a new standpoint.

This natural *ascesis* is undoubtedly of great value. It shows us to what extent body and mind affect each other. But is this actually prayer? Is not prayer something that God has given us in Jesus Christ? Certainly, Christian prayer is a more profound, more pervasive activity: calling upon the Father by the Son, thanking and extolling God the Father and praising Him together with Jesus. Body and mind, liberated by this exercise, come to spontaneous expression in it. Immediately, the individual has an inner sense of who it is to whom he has turned with his entire being. Words come to him of their own accord. Where they come from he does not know; but he recognizes them as *his* words. He may even just be silent. Silence, which is not a lack of words but transcends them, surpasses them, is a new form of dialogue in which we know only that the whole person is present. Presence in the most potent sense of the word, a being present in love that really does yield a knowledge of the other. And suddenly, out of the silence may arise at last a cry prompted in us by the Spirit. Our heart uncloses to exclaim: Abba, Father!

PRAYING—BUT WITH WHAT?

The main reason why prayer (and talking about prayer) seems so difficult nowadays is that we simply do not know what we are to pray *with*. Where in our body are we to locate the organ of prayer? Our lips and our mouth recite prayers, our intellect practises reflection and meditation, our heart and mind are lifted up to God. With this language we are familiar; but what is it we intend to convey by these concepts? Lips, mouth, intellect, heart and soul? What do we actually pray *with*?

The organ of prayer: our heart

Each person has been given by the creator an organ primarily designed to get him praying. In the creation story we read how God made man by breathing into him his living spirit (Gen. 2:7) and— St. Paul goes on—man became a living soul (I Cor. 15:45). Adam was the prefiguration of Him who should come: Jesus, the second Adam, after whose image the first man had been created. This means that being in relation with the Holy Trinity, Father, Son and Holy Spirit, is a fundamental part of our nature. The living spirit of God is the fount of prayer in us.

In the course of the centuries this organ has acquired very diverse names in various cultures and languages; but in fact they all signify the same thing. Let us agree to call it by the oldest name it has ever had—a name that in the Bible occupies a central place: the *heart*. In the Old Testament the heart denotes the inward man. The New Testament builds on this notion and perfects it.

The Lord it is who probes the heart and loins (Jer. 11:20), nothing is hidden from Him: Lord 'you examine me and know me, you know if I am standing or sitting ... God, examine me and know my heart, probe me and know my thoughts' (Ps. 139). The heart is what we yearn with: God grants the desire of the heart (Ps. 20:4). According to the Bible even a man's character is localized in this centre: out of the heart proceed thoughts, sins, good and bad inclinations: envy and malice, joy, peace and pity. The heart may also express the whole person, for instance, in Joshua's injunction to the Israelites regarding the occupation of the promised land: '... take great care to practise the commandments and the Law

16

which Moses the servant of Yahweh gave you: love Yahweh your God, follow his paths always, keep his commandments, be loyal to him and serve him with all your heart and soul' (Josh. 22:5).

But a part of the chosen people do not heed this call and turn their heart away from the Lord: '... this people approaches me only in words, honours me only with lip-service while its heart is far from me' (Isa. 29:13). The Israelites have hardened their hearts (Ezek. 2:14). Time after time God raises up prophets who will persist in speaking of this apostasy: 'But now, now—it is Yahweh who speaks—come back to me with all your heart, fasting, weeping, mourning. Let your hearts be broken, not your garments torn' (Joel 2:12), for the Lord cannot countenance such disloyalty. He loves Israel with an everlasting love, is a jealous God. And the prophets show us how even the heart of God is turned and his mercy (heart's compassion) is aroused (cf. Hosea 11:8). Never will His love desert His people: 'I did forsake you for a brief moment, but with great love will I take you back. In excess of anger, for a moment I hid my face from you. But with everlasting love I have taken pity on you, says Yahweh, your redeemer!' (Isa. 54:7-8).

At the very moment when the Jewish people are in deepest misery—the Babylonian exile—the prophet Ezekiel announces a new covenant: 'I shall pour clean water over you and you will be cleansed; I shall cleanse you of all your defilement and all your idols. I shall give you a new heart, and put a new spirit in you; I shall remove the heart of stone from your bodies and give you a heart of flesh instead. I shall put my spirit in you ...' (Ezek. 36:25-27).

Only a heart of flesh can really beat, can give life to the whole body. Only into such a heart can the Spirit make his entry; and the heart, at one time closed to the superabundance of grace, opens up again to His loving design: his Will, the Word, the Spirit.

He of whom Moses wrote in the Law—and the prophets also—Jesus, the son of Joseph of Nazareth, brought us this New Covenant. God Himself has intervened to open up the human heart and make it once more receptive to His Word (Acts 16:14). Ascended now into heaven, He has sent us another Paraclete ('Advocate': John 14:16), who consoles, strengthens and encourages, the Anointing who teaches us everything (I John 2:27), the Holy Spirit who will remind us of all that Jesus has said to us (John 14:26). 'If your lips confess that Jesus is Lord and if you believe in your heart that God raised him from the dead, then you will be saved' (Rom. 10:9). Heart and lips, inward surrender and outward confession, beat here to one and the same rhythm. And here, eventually, prayer is born.

The beatitudes sum up in a few sentences the spiritual Law of the New Covenant: 'How happy are the poor in spirit; ... happy those who mourn; ... happy the pure in heart: they shall see God' (Matt.

5:3–12). When nothing any longer clouds and darkens the heart, it can be wholly opened to the Light; for God is Love and God is Light.

It will perhaps be clear by now that the heart, in the ancient sense of the word, is not the discursive intelligence with which we reason, nor the 'feelings' with which we respond to another person, nor yet the superficial emotion we call sentimentality. The heart is something that lies much deeper within us, the innermost core of our being, the root of our existence or, conversely, our summit, what the French mystics call 'the very peak of the soul' ('la fine pointe de l'âme' or 'la cime de l'esprit'). In our everyday life our heart is usually concealed. It hardly reaches the surface of our consciousness. We much prefer to stay put in our outward senses, in our impressions and feelings, in all that attracts or repels us. And should we opt to live at a deeper level of our personal being, then we usually land up in abstraction: we reflect, we combine, we compare, we draw logical conclusions. But all this time our heart will be asleep—not beating yet to the rhythm of the Spirit.

Jesus was often reprimanding us: our hearts are blind, obdurate and closed (Mark 8:17). They are sluggish and slow (Luke 24:25), full of darkness, weighed down with pleasure and sorrows (Matt. 13:15). Our hearts must be circumcised. 'Circumcise your heart then, to love the Lord your God and serve Him with all your heart and your soul' (Deut. 10:12–22). Then love of God and of our neighbour will be the fruit, for a sound heart produces good fruit (Matt. 7:17). It is a main enterprise for every individual to find the way back to his heart. He is an explorer, moving into that unknown, inner region. He is a pilgrim in search of his heart, of his deepest being. Everyone carries within him—to repeat the marvellous expression used by St. Peter in his first letter—'the hidden man of the heart' (3:4). That 'man' is our deepest and most real being: he is who and what we *are*. There God meets us; and it is only from there that we in our turn can encounter people. There God addresses us; and from there we too are able to address people. There we receive from Him a new and as yet unfamiliar name, which He alone knows and which will be our name for ever in his Love; and only thence are we at length able to name another's name, in the selfsame Love.

But so far we have not reached that point. We are only on the road towards our heart. Still, the marvellous world that awaits us there makes taking the greatest trouble worthwhile.

In a state of prayer

For our heart is already in a *state of prayer*. We received prayer along with grace, in our baptism. The state of grace, as we call it, at the level of the heart, actually signifies a *state of prayer*. From then on, in the profoundest depths of the self, we have a continuing

18

contact with God. God's Holy Spirit has taken us over, has assumed complete possession of us; he has become breath of our breath and Spirit of our spirit. He takes our heart in tow and turns it towards God. He is the Spirit, Paul says, who speaks without ceasing to our spirit and testifies to the fact that we are children of God. All the time, in fact, the Spirit is calling within us and He prays, Abba-Father, with supplications and sighs that cannot be put into words but never for an instant cease within our hearts (Rom. 8:15; Gal. 4:6).

This *state of prayer* within us is something we always carry about, like a hidden treasure of which we are not consciously aware—or hardly so. Somewhere our heart is going full pelt, but we do not feel it. We are deaf to our praying heart, love's savour escapes us, we fail to see the light in which we live.

For our heart, our true heart, is asleep; and it has to be woken up, gradually—through the course of a whole lifetime. So it is not really hard to pray. It was given us long since. But very seldom are we conscious of our own prayer. Every technique of prayer is attuned to that purpose. We have to become conscious of what we have already received, must learn to feel, to distinguish it in the full and peaceful assurance of the Spirit, this prayer rooted and operative somewhere deep inside us. It must be brought to the surface of our consciousness. Little by little it will saturate and captivate our faculties, mind and soul and body. Our psyche and even our body must learn to answer to the rhythm of this prayer, be stirred to prayer from within, be incited to prayer, as dry wood is set ablaze. One of the Fathers puts it as tersely as this: 'The monk's ascesis: to set wood ablaze.'[1]

Prayer then, is nothing other than that unconscious *state of prayer* which in the course of time has become completely conscious. Prayer is the *abundantia cordis*, the abundance of the heart, as the saying goes in the Gospels: 'For a man's words flow out of what fills his heart' (Matt. 12:34; Luke 6:45). Prayer is a heart that overflows with joy, thanksgiving, gratitude and praise. It is the *abundance* of a heart that is truly awake.

Waking up

One condition is therefore that our heart comes awake; for as long as it remains asleep, our search for the organ of prayer in ourselves will be in vain. We can try to come at it in various ways; but the result will often be disconcerting. Some will put most reliance on their imagination; but there is a considerable risk of their ending up distracted and full of daydreams. Others may try through their religious feeling, but soon get bogged down in sentimentality. Yet others resort more to their intellect and try to arrive at clearer insights; but their prayer remains arid and cold and eventually ends up outside the sphere of their concrete living. Imagination, feeling and intellect are not of the Evil One. But they can only bear fruit when, much deeper within us, our heart comes to awakening and they, fed by the flame of this spiritual fire, themselves begin to glow.

Each and every method of prayer has but one objective: to find the heart and alert it. It must be a form of interior alertness, watchfulness. Jesus himself set 'being awake' and 'praying' side by side. The phrase 'be awake and pray' certainly comes from Jesus in person (Matt. 26:41; Mark 13:33). Only profound and quiet concentration can put us on the track of our heart and of the prayer within it.

All the time watchful and alert, therefore, we must first recover the way to our heart in order to free it and divest it of everything in which we have incapsulated it. With this in view we must mend our ways, come to our senses, get back to the true centre of our being as 'person', *redire ad cor* (Isa. 46:8), return to the heart, as people in the Middle Ages liked to say. In the heart, mind and body meet, it is the central point of our being. Once back at that central point, we live at a deeper level, where we are at peace, in harmony with everything and everybody, and first and foremost with our own self. This 'reversion' is also 'intro-version', a turning inward to the self. It engenders a state of recollection and interiority. It pierces through to our deepest 'I', to the image of God in us. To that ontological centre where we are constantly springing from God's creative hand and flowing back into His bosom. Praying teaches us to live from within, from the life within us. As was said of St. Bruno, every man of prayer has a *cor profundum*, a bottomless heart.[2] The parable of the prodigal son has been interpreted by several of the Fathers in that sense (Luke 15:11-32). The younger son demands his share of the estate and leaves for a distant country, where he squanders his money on a life of debauchery. 'When he had spent it all, that country experienced a severe famine and now he began to feel the pinch ... Then he came to his senses (literally: he turned in to his self) and said: "How many of my father's paid servants have more food than they want." ' Pope Gregory the Great applies the passage to St. Benedict, the father of western monasticism, whose life as a monk he thus describes: 'Had the prodigal son been with himself, whence then should he have returned to himself? Conversely, I might say of this venerable man (Benedict) that he dwelt with himself (habitare secum), for watching constantly over himself, he remained always in the presence of his Creator. He examined himself incessantly and did not allow his heart to divert its gaze to outward things.'[3] The passage shows us where St. Benedict's tranquillity came from. He does not seek to escape in an activity that will keep him away from his true work, but keeps on turning to his heart. There lies his true work: the battle with everything that would distract him from his sole Good. A twelfth-century Carthusian monk could say, therefore: Nothing makes the monk wearier than not working (Nihil laboriosius est quam non laborare)[6] and so continuing always free for prayer, finding his rest in Jesus and in his Word. Again, the same Carthusian says: in this way he comes to be *quietus Christo*, still and tranquil before Christ. This was Benedict's sole care also: to keep his heart free beneath the gaze of Him who offers both support and love.

To this ascesis—and especially the practice of keeping vigil—as a technique of prayer we shall return later on. Here we shall content ourselves with emphasizing that prayer has already been given us in our heart, albeit in a secret way. One cannot help but recall here the image of the treasure in the field. The application of it to prayer has indeed been made. A twelfth-century Cistercian, Guerric d'Igny, compares the heart to a field. The field of the heart must be dug over: 'O what precious store of good works, what a wealth of spiritual fruits are hidden in the field of a man's body and how much more, even, in his heart, if he will but dig and delve it. In so saying I do not mean to affirm with Plato that prior to its dwelling in this body, the soul already had knowledge which having been utterly forgotten and covered beneath a weight of sins is then laid bare by spiritual study (disciplina) and ascesis (labor). But I mean that reason and intelligence, which are peculiar to man, can when assisted by grace become the source of all good works. If thus you will *turn in your heart*, keeping your body under control, do not despair of finding therein treasures of sufficient worth' (Sermon 1 for Epiphany). There is a treasure, then, hidden in the field of our heart; and like the merchant of the gospel story we must sell all that we have in order to possess that field and extract the treasure from it. From time to time God allows us a glimpse of that treasure. Much effort will be needed to till the field. Our business here is not with exploiting the earth, entrusted by the Creator to the first man—a mandate that is certainly still in force. But still the sweat of our brow is required for exploiting the inner man and cultivating this fallow soil. Yet our toil will be rewarded—and more than that: this spiritual labour is itself a joy and gives us true peace.

Anyone whose heart has thus been freed will be able to listen in to it: the heart is at prayer, even without our knowing it. We can surprise our heart, as it were, in the very act of prayer. The spirit of Jesus anticipates us, is stammering our prayer before us. To give ourselves over to this prayer we have to yield ourselves and stop throwing up a barrier between our heart and our 'I'. We are not our 'persona', the *image* that we take so much trouble to create. Only when we have dropped this mask in the presence of God will we go on to uncover our real 'I'. And we shall stare in astonishment then; for could we ever have suspected what we were *really* like and what God had chosen for us? How fine, how beautiful, our true likeness is, which God carries with Him all the time and which He so much longs to show us! Out of love He has had respect for what we willed and has chosen to wait. This likeness can only be the likeness to his Son, who in advance of us lived out a true sonship and was obedient to the Father's will, right up to death on the cross. From His prayer, from His striving, living and dying, we learn how to pray.

Little by little we must advance on the road to prayer. The technique is always the same. To rid our heart of its surrounding dross; to listen to it where it is already at prayer; to yield ourselves to that prayer until the Spirit's prayer becomes our own.

As a monk of the Byzantine period once taught: 'Anyone who attends carefully to his heart, letting no other notions and fantasies get in, will soon observe how in the nature of things his heart engenders light. Just as coals are set ablaze and the candle is kindled by the fire, so God sets our heart aflame for contemplation, He who since our baptism has made our heart His dwelling-place.'[5]

Another monk of that period used a different metaphor to say the same thing. He was to an extraordinary degree a man of prayer, someone absolutely carried away by prayer, which was his constant occupation. He was asked how he had reached that state. He replied that he found it hard to explain. 'Looking back,' he said, 'my impression is that for many, many years I was carrying prayer within my heart, but did not know it at the time. It was like a spring, but one covered by a stone. Then at a certain moment Jesus took the stone away. At that the spring began to flow and has been flowing ever since.'

Third Chapter

THE PRAYER OF JESUS

The disciples felt a strong desire to pray when they saw Jesus praying. His prayer was infectious: 'Lord, teach us to pray' (Luke 11:1). They could not have wanted for opportunity. Jesus must have prayed very frequently. Echoes of this are to be heard in the New Testament record. There were times when He even spent the whole night in prayer (Luke 6:12), entirely alone in the solitude of some mountain. The evangelist shows how prior to every major event in Jesus' public life He would first spend time in prayer. It is Luke's Gospel in particular that stresses this. We read there how before appointing twelve disciples to be apostles Jesus prepared Himself in prayer. On another occasion Jesus chooses three disciples to whom for a brief moment He will reveal his glory. He takes them up a mountain; they leave behind them the noise and bustle of the world and journey into solitude (Luke 9:28-36).

It is not just that Jesus' prayer took up a substantial part of his time. His prayer as such is something quite out of the ordinary, something unutterably novel. Never has a human being been able to pray as Jesus did. For the very first time a human utterance acquired on His lips the fulness of its meaning. For the very first time also, the Father listened to words uttered by a human being, who actually is His very own Son, words that matched His boundless love in the most human fashion.

Indeed, the prayer of Jesus is closely associated with the fact that Jesus was at one and the same time God and man, that in Him the Word had become flesh; so that His prayer as man will embody and express something of what goes on in the life of the holy Trinity: the ineffable bond of complete harmony between Father and Son. Word and response, Love and answering Love, Gift and Gift-in-Return. The Son who has His primal source in the Father, dwells without intermission in the Father's bosom ('is nearest to the Father's heart': John 1:18) and is for ever returning into that source.

In the prayer of Jesus this divine reality is present in a unique way: The Love of which in His person He enshrines the fulness, the Will of the Father which is His only food, the Holy Spirit whom He receives from the Father. Until the coming of Jesus prayer was of necessity always suspended within a very restricted horizon. It had not yet come of age. In Jesus it can speak without reserve, and at once reaches its fullest, highest completion.

This was not so easy, however, as might appear at first sight. Not just because human words are deficient in themselves and because it was naturally difficult, therefore, for this ineffable, divine reality to create a suitable language. The difficulty lay much deeper. The human nature with which Jesus was invested still bore the traces of sin; and the language which He falteringly learnt to speak as a small boy also bore the stamp of sin. It was not pure, not as the Word of God is, 'nature's silver, without alloy, coming from the earth seven times refined' (Ps. 11:7), nor like prayer, re-creating the human words.

Just as Jesus had as it were to capture His perfect being-as-man in the teeth of our sin, so through stunted human words He had to battle for His prayer against our refusal. As a human being, even He had to *learn* to pray. And that He could only do where He came closest to our sin: namely, in temptation.

Temptation

It is impossible to write about prayer without discussing sin and temptation. After all, no other prayer is possible to human beings but the prayer that 'calls from the depths' (Ps. 129:1) of frailty, a prayer tangential to the circle of sin. Tangential because it simultaneously touches sin, and at the very same moment breaks through the boundary of sin and escapes from its cycle, in a burst of loving trust and confidence in the Lord, who alone can give release from temptation. 'Be awake and pray, urged Jesus, pray not to be put to the test' (Matt. 26:41). And He uttered this saying at the very moment when He had just emerged from the gravest temptation of His life: the temptation that was to inaugurate His death.

Of course, Jesus was Himself not a sinful person. He Himself could not sin because He was God. Even so, as man He was faced with sin. That was inevitable. The human body that He had assumed was still 'sinful flesh' (Col. 1:22; Rom. 8:3). This too, could not have been otherwise. The whole of humanity, after all, was waiting for Jesus in order to be redeemed from this state of sin; which is why Jesus had to go some part of the way with people, and even approach very close to sin.

Only the mystery of God's 'exceeding great love', as Paul puts it (Eph. 2:4) can in any way justify the foolishness of such a venture. The earliest New Testament theology tried to shed light on this mystery by reference to the figure of the servant of Yahweh in deutero-Isaiah (Isa. 42:1-4; 49:1-3; 50:4-9; 52:13-53:12). Love impels Jesus to humble Himself, in a staggering act of condescension, ever lower and lower, until He is subject to men, subject to sinners. Thus is revealed God's love towards sinners. It assumes the

24

features of the Servant. Utterly patient and humble. God goes along with us as far as sin. In Jesus He empties Himself of Himself and becomes as it were a sinner with sinners. He let Himself be counted among the evildoers (Luke 24:7).

The earliest Christian vocabulary had to look around for a special set of terms with which to give some sort of expression to this mystery. The New Testament speaks of emptying (kenōsis), being humbled, being 'lowered'. So for instance in the christological hymn of Philippians 2:5-8, which is held to incorporate a pre-Pauline liturgical passage. Jesus was the image of God. In his very origin He possessed the form of God; but He has divested Himself of this, emptied Himself (ekenōsen). Thus He has become a Servant, the Servant of Yahweh. And become man. He became humbler yet. Being found in outward form as a man, He humbled Himself yet more by becoming obedient to death, to death on the cross. Because of that, God has in an ineffable way exalted Him and given Him the Name which is above every name.

At this precise moment Jesus had to do with our sin. Not—I repeat—that there was any sin in Him. The Letter of John is explicit about that: 'there is no sin in Him' (I John 3:5). Yet He took sin upon Him—in the twofold sense of the verb *to bear* in Hebrew and Greek as well as in Latin (nasa, airein, tollere): *to bear* and *to bear away*. He loaded the sin upon Himself in order to take it away. In another place Paul makes use of an even bolder play on words: 'For our sake God made the sinless One into sin, so that in Him we might become the goodness of God' (2 Cor. 5:21). The pun here relates to the dual meaning of the Greek word for *sin* (hamartia): both *sin* and *expiatory sacrifice* or *peace-offering for sin*. The implication is then that although He was not a sinner, the Father has made Him a propitiatory sacrifice for sin. What is evident from all this, however, is that even Jesus had to struggle with sin, that at some point He was connected with sin. We can infer from that that even His prayer must in some respects be the tangent between sin and mercy: that is, between *our* sin, of which He as man bore the consequences in His own person, and the mercy of the Father, of which, again as man, He was the complete revelation. The prayer of Jesus is all of a piece with His task as Redeemer. He is a second Adam. That is to say: as man among men, with all His humanity and with all of humanity, He has to find the way back to the Father. The same path that the first Adam refused to take and that is now barred by the angel with the flaming sword (Gen. 3:24) Jesus will be the first to tread. Just where Adam failed, Jesus will try to break the barrier down.

Jesus then is the *Archègos* (Heb. 2:10), the Leader who goes out in front. He is the true *Prodromos* (Heb. 6:20), the Forerunner; the *Episkopos* (1 Peter 2:25), He who takes the lead (literally, the

25

overseer); the *Prōtotokos* (Rev. 1:5), the First-born. In the full sense of the word He is the *Prōtos*, as the Apocalypse calls Him, (Rev. 1:17), simply and solely the *First*. The first man of God's new creation: First-born of His marvellous Love. That is why Jesus takes the lead also in prayer and in the struggle that man must sustain in order to recover prayer. He is the first true Pray-er and from Him alone can we learn to pray. For that reason Jesus finds Himself having to face temptation. For to reopen the way to the Father for mankind He must first Himself stand upon that path. This is 'the way of all flesh', as it is called, the way of our humanity and of sinful flesh. He had to become wholly like us; for as the Fathers from Athanasius on are always saying: 'What He did not take upon Him He did not redeem.' Thus He even entered upon the world of sin and proceeded to live and die in the domain of sin itself. He took a human body, a body upon which sin was operative, with all the consequences that that entailed. This He did so that He could defeat sin on its own ground.

This comes out clearly in the Letter to the Hebrews: 'Since all the children share the same blood and flesh, he too shared equally in it, so that by his death he could take away all the power of the devil, who had power over death' (Heb. 2:14). In the flesh and blood of his human mode of being, Jesus had to confront the devil and to do so in death, that is, on the very ground which the devil himself controlled. For that reason Jesus had to undergo the great temptation of death, in order by His death to conquer the devil and redeem mankind. In Jesus, death was made to open on to life. It is no longer a death unto death, at least for the person who believes in Jesus. It is a death unto eternal life. The way to the Father is open again. For now Jesus Himself, in His risen body, is the Way (John 14:6). No one comes to the Father except through Him.

He became man, therefore, and not an angel (Heb. 2:14–18). Ordinary, run-of-the-mill man, like all other men, and so hedged around like them with weakness (Heb. 5:2). Again, He was faced with temptation so that He could become an understanding and merciful High Priest who has Himself been through the ordeal and is therefore in a position to help those who are tempted in their turn (Heb. 2:18). 'For it is not as if we had a high priest who was incapable of feeling our weaknesses with us; but we have one who has been tempted in every way that we are, though he is without sin' (Heb. 4:15).

Jesus' whole life was a temptation and a confrontation with the 'Prince of this world' (John 12:31). The innumerable cures that He performed, the resuscitations which He begged of His Father, the devils which He threw out of possessed people—these were so many signs of His struggle with evil. Likewise His prayer, which He sometimes continued in throughout the whole night, and which we may safely assume never really to have ceased. 'The fact is', Jesus declared to His disciples, 'there are devils which can only be cast out by prayer and fasting' (Matt. 17:21). This struggle with the devil had its climaxes in the major temptations forming a framework to the public ministry of Jesus: the temptation during the forty days' fast in the wilderness, and the final temptation within the Paschal mystery itself, with its two stages: the Mount of Olives and the death on the cross.

We must pause just for a moment and take a look at these temptations. After all, when Jesus underwent them He was praying all the time. His agony—even His death-agony—was an agony of prayer. And the surrender to the Will of His Father, which was the outcome of each temptation, in other words His obedience, was an obedience of prayer. His sacrifice too, which as High Priest He offered up in the temptation and the victory, was a sacrifice of prayer. The selfsame sacrifice which He now celebrates perpetually in Glory. At this very moment He is 'living for ever to intercede' (Heb. 7:25).

Obedience in prayer

One cannot talk about prayer without also referring to obedience. By obedience we do not mean here the sociological kind of obedience relevant to the life of any group, whatever the nature of that group may be. To further the good of the group each member will feel morally bound to obey the responsible person who together with the rest but in a special manner, has to point to the good of the group and convert it into concrete instructions. Of course we have no objection to bring against this sort of obedience, the need for which is immediately obvious wherever a group, even a religious group, wants to survive and be effective.

Here however, we mean by obedience something else: the giving up of one's own longings and desires—My will—for the Will of another—Your Will—specifically in this case the Will of the Father. This surrendering of oneself, this setting aside of one's own desires in favour of someone else, of another, puts the one who obeys in a new relationship to that Other. Obedience is a language and a sign. It also effects something in the one who obeys. It lays his life entirely open to the requirements of an Other and binds him fast to that Other. More, much more even than that. It can engender new life. By laying someone open to an Other, it alters him in the deepest sense of the word. It is a new life-style, whereby a person can detach himself more and more from his own constricted state, so as to be engrossed in the richness of an Other and to share that richness with Him. This is assuming, of course, that the obedience is spontaneous and free and never degenerates into slavery. This calls for a pure love and a great love on both sides.

Of His Father's love Jesus was totally sure. In His divine person, therefore, no hesitation regarding His Father's Will is possible. He is indeed *Amen*, as the Apocalypse calls Him (Rev. 3:14), which is to say: Yes, Father (Matt. 11:26). With His whole being He assents to His Father's Love. Thus He can even say that here below He has no other food than to do the Will of His Father (John 4:34). That is His reason for becoming man (John 6:38). But here the difficulty begins. The Father gave His Son a body so that Jesus could act obediently as man—something that man since Adam had not been able to do. That obedience on Jesus' part, through His human body, is actually going to be *the* Sacrifice of the New Covenant. According to the Letter to the Hebrews Jesus said on coming into the world: 'You who wanted no sacrifice or oblation prepared a body for me ... God, here I am! I am coming to obey your will' (Heb. 10:5-7).

For Jesus this is to be a very painful experience; for our redemption consists precisely in the fact that His obedience as God now assumes a human form in a body and in a psychology marked by sin. Jesus is to be engulfed by this drama, is to die and rise again. As soon as He as much as tries to live out that obedience in His human condition, it bursts apart. His body defaults, He exudes water and blood, He dies. Only the Father can save Him from that death and embody in Him the underlying meaning of all obedience. He calls Him back to life, He invests His body with His own Glory.

This bloody confrontation with His Father's Will in His human body ran right through the prayer: 'not My will but Your Will be done!' (Matt. 26:39). Jesus fought that battle in constant prayer; and He was answered through and beyond death. His prayer could only be a cry for obedience, and His obedience was all that He could pray. Deep within Jesus, the Will of the Father was at one with His most fervent longing to pray. Jesus was Himself, in His most intimate relationship to His Father, in the very core of His being: obedience-in-prayer. This obedience we find in one of the most familiar sentences of the prayer which He Himself taught to His disciples: Your Will be done on earth as in Heaven.

To penetrate even further into the obedience of Jesus and the mystery of His prayer, let us pause for a moment to consider that Will of the Father to which Jesus is prepared to surrender His own will. Do we really understand what the Will of the Father implied for Jesus? The very idea 'Will of God' prompts a certain amount of resistance nowadays, especially when used in connection with obedience. For many years past the expression has been used in the modern vernaculars, in a limited perspective difficult to adapt to the biblical notion of obedience. Nowadays the human will is taken to denote a faculty identifiable with neither intellect nor feeling. In Dutch, for instance, 'will' is associated with 'will-power', that is, with the ability to direct our emotional life and our need for affection into the right channels—and that, not without a certain amount of toughness and effort. 'Will' suggests something else to us as well: namely, a decision. 'I will have it so,' coming from a superior, means: 'I've decided on that; that's how it's going to be.' In that sort of context we can without knowing it slip into a false idea of the Will of God: a mysterious force that more or less constrains our intelligence and feelings, and may perhaps even thwart them; a decision, with all the arbitrary, capricious quality that this can imply; a command which I must carry out willy-nilly, even though we do not agree with it, even though it is alien to us and in no way concerns me. One cannot altogether deny that a type of spirituality current in the last century had turned 'the Will of God' into something as capricious and menacing as the sword of Damocles hanging over one's head, something that one was not going to escape and that would strike in one's most unguarded moment.

The biblical notion of the Will of God bears very little resemblance indeed to that. What the Vulgate translates as *voluntas* and *beneplacitum* goes back to the Greek *thèlèma* or *eudokia*. Both terms render the Hebrew *rasôn* (and sometimes *hps*). Now the ambience of these terms is quite different: longing, desire, love, joy. Then again, being 'in love' and the sexual desire that a man feels for a woman are denoted by the same concepts.

Thus the Love (Will) of God rests upon the people that He has chosen for Himself in His good pleasure. The prophet Isaiah uses the same terms with which to celebrate the salvation of Mount Zion: 'You are to be a crown of splendour in the hand of Yahweh, a princely diadem in the hand of your God; no longer are you to be named "Forsaken", nor your land "Abandoned", but you shall be called "My Delight" and your land "The Wedded"; for Yahweh takes delight in you and your land will have its wedding. Like a young man marrying a virgin, so will the one who built you wed you, and as the bridegroom rejoices in his bride, so will your God rejoice in you' (Isa. 62:3–5). My *delight* stands for the same Hebrew word that the Vulgate persistently renders by *voluntas-Will*. So the *Will of God* here signifies the pleasure the Lord takes in His people, the great love that He feels for His chosen ones. This is His *thèlèma*, His *Will*: that He should love the Jewish people despite the many times they have been disloyal.

The fulness of that same Love now rests upon Jesus. He is the desire of His Father, His Delight. In Him the Father as it were finds repose. This is undoubtedly the gist of the all but solitary saying that the Father utters in the New Testament. It was meant for Jesus. He heard it at His baptism and at His transfiguration. In this saying the Father said all that He had to say. All other utterances are left to Jesus. We find it, with a few variants, in Matt. 3:17 and

17:5; in Mark 1:11; in Luke 3:22 and in the Second Letter of Peter 1:17. In translation: 'You are My Son, My Beloved; My favour rests on You.' Behind the Greek verb *eudokein* here there undoubtedly stands the semitic *rasôn* (which is also rendered by *thèlèma-Will*). Thus the Father is here bearing witness that the fulness of His Will—in the sense of Love, longing, delight—rests upon His well-beloved Son.

So Jesus Himself is the place *par excellence* where God reveals Himself, the human being in whom the *thèlèma*, the yearning, the love and the Will of the Father are made plain. Jesus is the epiphany of the Father's pleasure, the Father's joy. How could it be otherwise? Was He not born before all ages from the bosom of His Father, born of His deepest desire and His abounding love? Now, in the fulness of time, the well-beloved Son has united Himself with what is essentially human. This being born of the Father He must now express in human fashion. This is to be His obedience. He must allow this Father-love to flow through His whole being-as-man. It must occupy and capture His human body and His entire psychology. In that way the Father's Love will be realized and endorsed. Where the first man had said No, Jesus, the new Man, will say Yes. He will make the Will of the Father wholly His own. He has to become the first man in whom the fulness of God's love can become a reality. That is His obedience, that is also His death. And these two are His Love. So too is His prayer. It is noteworthy that in both cases—that of Baptism and that of Transfiguration—this utterance, this Word of the Father, was a response to the prayer of Jesus. It is Luke, as usual, who is careful to mention this detail. While Jesus was praying, the heavens opened and the Father's voice rang out (Luke 3:21). And He was again at prayer when His countenance was suddenly altered and his clothes became white as snow (Luke 9:29). His prayer was at the same time a loving surrender to the Will of His Father, and a further disclosure of that same Will.

The most painful confrontation with the Will of the Father took place in the garden of Gethsemane. Here the prayer and the struggle took on a bloody aspect. In many very ancient manuscripts the most realistic verses of this Lucan pericope (22:43-44) have been squeamishly omitted. Many a copyist must have wavered and jibbed at the representation of so much suffering. As to the authenticity of the deleted passage, however, there can be no serious doubt. It was a cruel moment for Jesus. The Angel of Yahweh has to intervene, as he had done in the Old Testament at the crucial moments in Israel's history, especially on the field of battle. Truth to tell, Jesus struggles as He prays: 'And being seized with mortal anguish, He prayed even more fervently.' The word *agōnia* has a twofold meaning here: anguish, misery, desperation; but also struggle. Neither meaning should be disregarded here. Jesus finds Himself embroiled in the decisive struggle and in great anguish—in both to the point of death. It is the struggle of obedience but also of prayer. A battle of prayer and obedience in prayer. As He prays, Jesus will receive obedience from His Father and wring it, as it were, from His body. The more fervently He prays, the more does His bloody sweat drip to the ground. Jesus is committed to this battle, body and soul; and He discovers how feeble man's flesh is, however fervent and however potent the spirit may be.

The New Testament has preserved yet another account of this crucial struggle; and it is no less realistic. Once again we find, side by side, the battle, the obedience and the prayer. But a new and important element appears: as He prays and as He struggles, Jesus is made an anointed priest. The passage in question is found in the Letter to the Hebrews 5:7-10: 'During his life on earth, he offered up prayer and entreaty, aloud and in silent tears, to the one who had the power to save him out of death, and he submitted so humbly that his prayer was heard. Although he was Son, he learnt to obey through suffering; but having been made perfect, he became for all who obey him the source of eternal salvation and was acclaimed by God with the title of high priest of the order of Melchizedek.'

The passage gives us the priestly terminology of the Letter to the Hebrews. Jesus *offered up* (*prosferein*) prayers. His obedience and His death on the cross were a sacrifice, a high-priestly action. More than that. In this obedience and in this sacrifice of prayer He was *anointed priest* (*teleiôtheis* in the special meaning of this word throughout the Letter) and as such 'acclaimed' by the Father. This came about in suffering and temptation. From what He suffered, the author says, He *learned* obedience, even though He was Himself the Son of God. As man, however, as we have already seen, He had to wrest that obedience from our sin. We can say the same of prayer. In this temptation Jesus *learnt* to pray. *Only* there, that is to say, and only as man was He able to wrest His prayer and His Word of Assent from our denial. He had to learn from this hopelessness and desperation and from death. Only loud entreaty and tears—the prayer of extreme desolation—could scoop out in the man Jesus, those bottomless depths of surrender and obedience in which ultimately the Will of God, that is, the Father's Love, could be fully realized. How great the temptation was and by what a narrow margin Jesus overcame it we can to some extent infer from the cry of despair which like the Psalmist He lets fall from His lips: 'My God, My God, why have You deserted me?' Jesus suddenly senses the absurdity of His death and how incomprehensible His Father's attitude is. This is the temptation of despair. The soldiers could not understand that cry. They thought that He was calling upon Elijah. Few at that moment would have had any inkling of what was going on inside Him. Perhaps Our Blessed Lady beneath the cross and St.

John, the disciple whom He loved? He was not invoking Elijah but was asking His own Father why He had left Him alone. That is the dark question of the human race, after Adam's No. In the voice of Jesus, Adam's despair is uttered, that despair which Jesus had always carried as a potentiality in His human body and which in the senseless face of death suddenly threatened to get the upper hand.

Would Jesus then actually reach the point of doubting His Father's love? The evangelists have not put that doubt into His mouth. But we can detect it in the pointed ridicule the high priests and scribes fling at Him from beneath the cross: 'He puts His trust in God. Let God deliver Him now, if *He takes delight in Him*. For He said: I am the Son of God!' (Matt. 27:43). This is the most hurtful abuse, and the worst temptation. On His cross Jesus hears once more the only words that the Father had addressed to Him here on earth, the declaration of His Love. But He hears it now on the lips of His own enemies, as a taunt and a reproach.

And yet the Father will save Him; for in the teeth of all human hope Jesus is going to believe that despite everything the Father loves Him. Not apart from death, not in a detour around death, but right through death, to a new life. This is what He has to learn from suffering and death. That the Father loves Him right up to death and to life eternal. In the end it is only in death that Jesus as man could learn just how much the Father did love Him. Only in this immense ordeal, on the edge of such despair, could Jesus at prayer utter His Yes to the Will of the Father. Only at *that* point, even as He was dying, could He obey: 'Father, into your hands I commit my spirit' (Luke 23:46; Ps. 31:6).

Those words which He borrows from the same psalmist mean that He lets Himself go and slide away into death. A dying person is always prone to cling fast to what he thinks is life. Jesus too, experienced that inevitable, as it were, ontological convulsive reflex which in every man is a trace of sin, and prevents him from advancing into the new life that must be given birth and come to light in death. In total surrender and utter defencelessness, without seeing, without knowing, in spite of the sense of going to destruction and being devoured by death, Jesus lets Himself go ... into the hands of His Father.

For His end is not in death but in Love. And He proffers to His Father His own *spirit*, that is to say, His *ruah*, the most intimate thing that a person receives from God, his breath of life. What an individual passes on to others in a kiss of love, Jesus as He dies gives back here to His Father in an ultimate embrace. All at once He discovers the response to His Father's declaration of love: 'You are My Son, My Well-beloved. All My favour rests on You.' It took Jesus His whole life as a man to get through to the deepest reality of these words. And only now does he know. Only now can He *really* pray. Only in death will He be able to utter in its fulness the long matured Yes of His own Love for the Father, to speak it in peace, beyond all despair and doubt. His prayer is the loving kiss in which He breathes His last: 'Father, into your hands I commit my spirit.'

Had Jesus given in to that temptation, we would have remained in death for ever, and the way to prayer would for ever have been barred. Now that way is open and free again. He Himself is the Way ... and the Life (John 14:6).

'Living for ever to intercede' (Heb. 7:25)

This was Jesus' task as High Priest of the New Covenant, as Mediator between His Father and sinful humanity: that He should be the first to restore access to the Holy of Holies. That way He prepared and that Way He Himself trod. Just as once a year the Jewish High Priest would pass through the veil into the Holy of Holies, so once for all did Jesus enter the Holy of Holies through the veil of the new temple. That veil—the author of the Letter to the Hebrews observes (Heb. 10:20)—was His own flesh, through which He passed as He died and rose again; so that His own body, raised from the dead, has become the 'new and living' Way whereby everyone now has access to the holy place.

The tent of the Covenant and the holy place are now quite different from what prefigured them in the Old Testament liturgy. They are 'far greater and more perfect, and not made by men's hands' (Heb. 9:11). The sanctuary is heaven itself and the throne of the Father, at whose right hand our High Priest is stationed in order to be an eternal Intercessor on our behalf (Heb. 9:24). The sacrifice of prayer—*sacrificium laudis*—which He was required to initiate in obedience and death, He now celebrates for ever in heaven. He is 'living for ever to intercede for us' (Heb. 7:25).

That is where Jesus is praying *now*, in the boundless present of the eternity which cannot be attained or embodied in our created time, unless it be in prayer. Thus Jesus is for ever the man of prayer, our interceding High Priest. In that, He is 'the same today as He was yesterday and as He will be for ever' (Heb. 13:8). Up above, in the risen Jesus, lies also the source of our prayer here below. As we pray, we can be there at His side, can, as it were, break through and surmount the limitations of time as we know it, breathe the air of eternity and stand with Jesus before the Father's face.

But to that end we must take the same Way here below that Jesus took, for there is no other Way: His cross, His death. The same Letter to the Hebrews observes that Jesus underwent His crucifixion outside the city gate. Christians too, therefore, are to 'go to Him outside the camp and share His degradation', that is, the

33

degradation of His cross. This going out to meet with Jesus is something that every baptized person carries as a deep yearning within his heart. 'For there is no eternal city for us in this life but we look for one in the life to come', where Jesus already is. And so are we, in so far as we remain with Him in prayer. 'Through Him let us offer God an unending sacrifice of praise, a verbal sacrifice that is offered every time we acknowledge His name.' For the Christian walking in the steps of Jesus offers up as He did a sacrifice of prayer. He acknowledges and calls unceasingly upon His name. He also shares everything with his brothers in love, as the same author goes on to say: 'Keep doing good works and sharing your resources, for these are sacrifices that please God.'

This short passage from the thirteenth chapter of the Letter to the Hebrews, which we have been considering in a cursory fashion here, describes the dual liturgy which every Christian today should never cease to celebrate. Both originate in the Sacrifice of Jesus and in the liturgy which He is continuously celebrating, as our priest, in the presence of His Father. On the one hand the sacrifice of prayer through which we constantly invoke His name and pray for all men; on the other hand the sacrifice of love, whereby we share the Father's gifts with all our brothers. This then is the new liturgy of those who, like Jesus, have taken the Way of obedience to the point of death and, beyond death, of Life. Of that Life and of that Glory there were already traces in the body of Jesus during His earthly life, but only at rare moments. The most striking instance of this is His Transfiguration. We remarked before how this took place in solitude, on a mountain, and while Jesus was praying. All at once the deep reality of His prayer assumed a visible form, in His body and His clothes, even in the natural world around Him. The cloud indicated how near God was; and the voice of the Father showed just how much He loved Him. In Moses and Elijah, representing the Law and the Prophets, the Old Testament was present to acknowledge the promised Messiah. And they speak with Jesus about the Exodus which He is soon to accomplish at Jerusalem, that is to say, about His death and resurrection.

The Church too is involved in the mystery of Jesus' prayer. On Mount Tabor she is present in the three favourite disciples. The whole event fills them with fear and awe. And yet it arouses in them a feeling of enormous regret, an insatiable craving to prolong and perpetuate this intimacy, to linger for ever with this glorified Jesus. No doubt Peter's reaction betrays a hunger in him for prayer; but it was at the same time an 'Exodus reflex'. The wish that Peter ventures to express on behalf of the three is a clear allusion to the Exodus and the ritual of the Feast of Tabernacles, in which each year the Jews liturgically celebrated the Exodus. Actually, tents were put up for all taking part, to remind them of the tents the people of God had used in the wilderness. Now Peter wants to erect such tents on this spot, one for Jesus, one for Moses and one for Elijah. Because it 'is good to be here', he spontaneously takes his place with Jesus in the Exodus. That is still the Church's deep desire today, especially when she looks to the Lord in prayer and is already close to Him.

Prayer begins, in the most literal sense, to light up in the very body of Jesus. His face radiates the Glory of God, the same Glory that as the Only-Begotten He had received from the Father 'before ever the world was' (John 17:5). All that is human about Him, yes, even His clothing, is steeped in the lustre of His divine nature, He appears enveloped in light and in fire. For God is light (1 John 1:5), and God is a consuming fire (Heb. 12:29).

The man of prayer may sometimes radiate in this transitory life the glory that he is to receive at his resurrection. For the incarnation of Jesus, His having become man, and the power of His glorious resurrection are already working at full stretch in our world. Admittedly, that power is still concealed, like the leaven in the dough (Matt. 13:33). Yet it may sometimes even now percolate through what is perishable and transient and grace a man with the splendour of the life to come. A well-known patristic adage pictures a monk surprised by another in the act of prayer: 'A brother came to the cell belonging to Prior Arsenius. He waited at the door and saw the Prior as it were a mass of fire. When he knocked the Prior opened and saw the disconcerted brother.'[1]

In a few simple sentences this anecdote tells how the prayer that burned in the heart of Arsenius consumed his whole body like fire. A flicker of the Glory that lights up the face of Jesus (2 Cor. 4:6), a participation in the uncreated Light that God Himself is (cf. Col. 1:12).

Fourth Chapter

THE LIVING WORD

Born of the Word

Jesus came among us to bear witness to the life that was with the Father, so that by believing in Him we might have eternal life. This is the work of God, the *Opus Dei*, in the strictest sense of the term. We have to believe in Him. He will then reveal, will then interpret to us all that He has seen the Father do. For Jesus and the Father are one, even when Jesus is proclaiming the Word of the gospel here on earth, even when He feels Himself deserted by everything and everybody. Even during His life among men He remained in union with the Father (although He was not always, in His human psychology, conscious of the fact). 'No one has ever seen God; it is the only Son, who is nearest to the Father's heart, who has made Him known' (John 1:18). Jesus is the *exegete* of the Father (in fact the Greek has *exegesato*, expressed in English as 'made known'). The life that was with the Father He has declared, made clear to us, so that our ears and eyes can grasp and understand it. The Word has put into words what cannot be uttered. By the Word the earth was created and all that is in it. 'In Him were created all things ... all things were created through Him and for Him' (Col. 1:16). For God spoke and it was so (Gen. 1:3). Since the creation is also a sign of God, it can be a pointer to Him. 'Ever since God created the world His everlasting power and deity—however invisible—have been there for the mind to see in the things He has made' (Rom. 1:20). The book of nature speaks of God, to anyone who knows how to use his eyes. But sin has set its mark on the creation; and as a result what was once a reflection of God's wisdom and omnipotence has now become clouded and obscure. Whereas at first everything spoke of God, God must now come to man's aid with His Word. He addresses mankind and wants to conclude a Covenant with it. First with Noah, then with Abraham whose faith was accounted to him for righteousness. Thus Abraham became the Father of all the faithful, as numerous as the grains of sand on the seashore. Moses carved the Ten Sayings on tablets of stone, the ten commandments which the Lord had delivered to him on Mount Sinai. There Moses had conversed with God, as friend with friend; and so he had been able to proclaim the Word of the Lord and become the prophet par excellence: 'Never has there been such a prophet in Israel as Moses, the man Yahweh knew face to face' (Deut. 34:10). After him the prophets will continue to speak the Word of the Lord and set everything that happens in a true light, in God's light. The Word creates and performs its work. 'Yes, as the rain and the snow come down from the heavens and do not return without watering the earth, making it yield and giving growth to provide seed for the sower and bread for the eating, so the Word that goes from my mouth does not return to me empty, without carrying out my will and succeeding in what it was sent to do' (Isa. 55:10–11). The whole of the Old Testament witnesses to this hankering after the Word that is to end the need for further words. In the fulness of time the Word is revealed and by being preached is spread throughout the whole earth, so that all who hear it may come to believe (cf. Rom. 10:17–18).

The word is carried forward and passed from person to person, from father to son. Before the Word can once more be imparted, it must first be wholly appropriated by us and made our own, taken into that inmost, profoundest part where God awakens a response to it and makes it prosper. Then when the Word is uttered, it is something of our very being that we impart. The Word of God proclaimed like *that* has become our word also. We have become part of the scheme of salvation. However meagrely, alas! the new life is being revealed in us.

'I tell you most solemnly, unless a man is born through water and the Spirit, he cannot enter the kingdom of God: what is born of the flesh is flesh; what is born of the Spirit is spirit' (John 3:5–6). Baptism with water and the Holy Spirit is the new birth. During the very early Christian centuries the candidate for baptism was immersed in an actual bath of water, he relived, as it were, the descent of Jesus into the bowels of the earth and His consequent rising to new life in the Light. All this was accompanied by a recital of the epiklesis, a prayer beseeching the Holy Spirit to descend upon the candidate and raise what has been immersed in the death of Jesus to new life. The individual becomes then and there a member of the new creation through the Spirit now given to him. The light of Christ—foretaste of his glory at the end of time—comes upon him. That is why in the New Testament letters baptized people are often referred to as 'those who have received the light' (Heb. 10:32). 'Wake up from your sleep, rise from the dead, and Christ will shine on you' (Eph. 5:14).

This being born again of water and the Word changes completely a man's inmost being. Nowadays baptism is administered, generally speaking, at a very tender age, when the baby has only been in the world for a few days. Thus evidences of an inner change at the time of baptism have become very few and far between. Yet at least once in his life every Christian must have an intense experience of this new reality. The grace of baptism will then be actualized in a special way. Anyone who goes through the experience will share in the light that comes from Christ. He himself and all around him will then assume a different complexion, a new aspect. A new vision will be his, enabling him to look at everything in the light of God. 'By your light we see the light' (Ps. 35:10). The created world, the people with whom he comes in contact, everything that lives, he can now envisage from a supernatural viewpoint. They take their place within that plan of salvation which God is so eager to implement. He waits only for a man to take one step in order to make yet a further offer of His grace and show him more of His Love. A Love heaped upon his head.

This rebirth is the achievement of the Word: St. Peter expresses it with complete assurance: '... your new birth was not from any mortal seed but from the everlasting Word of the living and eternal God' (1 Peter 1:23). The locus of that birth, the place where the Word comes to fruition in us, is the heart. The grace of baptism becomes actual when the Word of God addresses our heart for the first time. Here we come back to the organ of prayer within us. The Fathers use a wealth of expressions to describe this experience: the Word of God *touches* our heart, it *wounds*, it *needles*, it *pierces*, it *cleaves* our heart *open*. The Word *jolts* our heart *awake*. 'Wake up, sleeper' (Eph. 5:14). At the very centre of a man, at his core, in his heart, the new light arises. 'It is the same God that said, "Let there be light shining out of darkness," who has shone in our minds (hearts) to radiate the light of the knowledge of God's glory, the glory on the face of Christ' (2 Cor. 4:6).

Heart and Word

So first we have to get through to our heart. As we have already seen, prayer has already been sown in it, since our baptism. There, in our innermost 'I', Jesus is present. Everything that goes on outside our heart and, as it were, at the door of our heart, serves only to help uncover the treasure concealed within. There is the Easter tomb, and there the new life: 'Woman, why are you weeping? Whom are you looking for? The one you seek is in your possession, and you do not know it? You have the true, the eternal joy, and yet you weep? It is within your inmost being, and you look for it without? You stand outside, weeping at the tomb. Your heart is my tomb. And I am not dead there, but I take my rest in your heart, living for ever. Your soul is my garden. You were right to suppose that I was the gardener. I am the New Adam. I till and mind my paradise. Your tears, your love and your longing are all my work. In your inmost being you possess me, although you do not know it, and so you look for me without. Outwardly, therefore, I will appear to you, and so make you return to yourself, that in your inmost being you may find the one whom you seek outside.'[1] And our heart is best reached by way of the Word of God. On condition, however, that we let the Word of God really be what in all truth it is: a power of God (Rom. 1:16). And provided we set ourselves to the task with a heart denuded and with that alone. That is to say, we are to just let it quieten down and shut it off from all other preoccupations, be they theological, apologetic or even pastoral. For this meeting between the Word and the heart of a man is of one cannot say how much greater importance. Do we wake up or go on sleeping, shall we be born or shall we simply tail off in death—this, after all, is what is at stake. Our heart *alone*, therefore, must be laid bare to the creative and generative power of the Word of God; while our other faculties retreat for a time into silence and wait in patience.

'Speak, Lord, to the heart of your servant, that my heart may speak with You.'[2] This is the whole amazing mystery of God's Word, coming once again to its fulfilment in our heart. For a time our heart may slumber on; but God's Spirit is already present within it and unbeknown to us is crying out to the Father. The same Spirit of God is present also in God's Word that comes into our heart from outside. From the very outset there exists an affinity between the Word from outside, awakening us, and the Spirit watching and waiting in our sleeping heart. The heart of man was made to receive the Word, and the Word adapts itself to the dimensions of our human heart. The one is there for the other. The Word is sown in the heart (Matt. 13:19; Luke 8:12). But for that the heart must be cleansed (Matt. 5:8; Heb. 10:22) and made ready (Luke 8:15). For normally our heart is hardened and our spirit closed up (Mark 6:52; 8:17; John 12:40; Eph. 4:18; Heb. 3:8; 3:15; 4:7). It is dull and slow to believe (Luke 24:25). It is full of darkness (Rom. 1:21). It is easily weighed down with cares and pleasures (Luke 21:34). For these reasons it is unable to relish its spiritual food: the Word of God.

But when the Word of God accosts our heart, then suddenly and quite unexpectedly the one may recognize the other, thanks to the one Spirit who is present in both. A bridge is made, as it were, between our heart and the Word. From heart to Word a spark is transmitted. Between the Spirit lying dormant deep within our heart and the Spirit who is active in the Word a fruitful and vitalizing dialogue begins. Engendered from an imperishable seed (1 Peter 1:23), the heart is born again of the Word. We recognize in the Word, as in a mirror, our new countenance. By it we become witnesses to our rebirth in Christ (James 1:23). 'The hidden man of the heart' (1 Peter 3:4) awakens within us.

So the Word penetrates to the very depths of our being, like a sharp and two-edged sword, cleaving between soul and spirit, joints and marrow (Heb. 4:12) and generating new life in us. The Word lays our heart quite bare. Now, and only now, can our untrammelled heart really and truly proceed to listen to God's Word. Deeper and deeper it penetrates. Word and heart mirror each other and come to resemble each other more and more. The heart is aware of itself now as a new organ, with new senses and a sensibility previously unknown.

'Man does not live on bread alone but on every word that comes from the mouth of God' (Matt. 4:4). The Word of God comes to us in many different ways. A passage read out in church during a celebration of the eucharist may prepare us for receiving bread and wine changed by the power of the Word into the body and blood of Christ. It may be the Word of Scripture proclaimed to the brothers 'in full assembly' (Ps. 22:23). The Word may also be imparted to me by a brother or sister, just as the still unrecognized Jesus expounded the Scriptures to the two disciples on the road to Emmaus. 'Did not our hearts burn within us?' (Luke 24:32). It is a Word that can reverberate for each of us personally when we take the Bible with us into our own room and shut the door behind us in order to be alone with Jesus and his Word. It is a peculiar feature of this living Word that it is passed on, so to speak, from father to son. That is to say, the Word only reaches the baptized person via the living band of brothers and sisters who have been born of this same Word before him. This may be the role of a priest; but a lay person too, can be for us the spiritual father or mother through whom the Word comes to us and by whom the new life is brought to birth in our heart. This is the normal way of attaining to an awakened heart and the practice of prayer. You do not learn this on your own. You learn it from someone else. You may learn it from the look on another's face or catch the sound of it in his heart—in a heart that lives, that radiates life and awakens others to life.

In this process of spiritual direction—or counselling, as people rightly prefer to call it nowadays—Tradition, the Tradition, reaches its culminating point. Here Tradition becomes once again an existential process of handing on: Spirit and life brought to birth in someone else. This vitalizing contact with a *spiritual father* in the full sense of the term—by which I mean a father who is himself guided by the Holy Spirit and who is able to assist and counsel others in the Holy Spirit—is an essential element on the path to prayer. It is witness and it is dialogue. Witness, because the spiritual father renders account, as it were, to a brother for the life which the Lord has brought about in him: he speaks the Word of God, he passes it on. Dialogue, because the brother renders account to his spiritual father of his own spiritual aspirations. Thus the life of the Spirit which is slowly germinating and growing in the junior person is sustained by the same life which in a senior—an 'old one', a *staretz*, in the literal sense—has already come to full maturity.

So the spiritual father forms a living bond with the Tradition. It is now his turn to interpret the Word; and in this handing on of his experience the Word attains to new Life. We come to understand our vocation in it, and the Will of God concerning us. He will keep our prayer-life from going off the rails and will keep on bringing it back to the yardstick of the Word and to the objectivity of the Holy Spirit. Actually, according to the ancient texts, the spiritual father should be *pneumatophoros*, that is, a *carrier or vehicle of the Spirit*. In the Holy Spirit he understands from inside the mystery of prayer. He is totally familiar with the words of the Bible which are for him already 'spirit and life'. He helps us to listen out for the echo of this Word in our heart. Himself full of reverence and love for the work of God's Spirit, he makes us sensitive to its inner promptings and patiently sees to it that they gradually find their due expression in our life. He is at the same time father and mother, yes, and brother too, and equally that dearest friend who knows how to suffer with us and bears along with us the burden of our temptations, who—as Paul puts it—endures the pangs of childbirth until Christ is formed in us (Gal. 4:19); someone whose calm faith rebuts our cavils and our doubts; someone, finally, who is a living link between Christ and us, who at our side is witness to His love, someone to whom we might apply the words of Kierkegaard concerning his own father: 'From him I have learnt what a father's love is, and so I have got some idea of the fatherly love of God, the only unshakable thing in our lives, the true Archimedean point.'[3]

A lot of people in these days feel the need to be given a word. They are looking for somebody who can deliver such a word, who can stir up the Word within them. For in the first phase of his searching for God man has not yet received the Spirit. He cannot yet understand the Word of God, as he is still *unspiritual* (1 Cor. 2:14). Only he who has been taught by the Spirit of God, the *spiritual* person, knows the things of God and understands his Word. He is also able to exercise a *fatherhood-according-to-the-Spirit*: to hand on the Word and watch over and see to its growth. We must not underestimate the importance of this transferring of the Word. The process brings to us the Word of Creation that brought the universe into *being*. It is an echo of the first Word that God uttered over the world on the day when the first light appeared in the darkness. Still today it is the Word-of-the-Beginning, the Genesis-Word. Happy the man to whom it has been given to hear for himself, from the mouth of his spiritual father, this Word-of-the-Beginning. He already carries the new world in his heart. Whatever the paths by which the Word reaches us, only in our heart can it come to life and to its full growth; so we must apply ourselves to the Word with a tremendous desire for it. We must receive the Word like manna in the wilderness and not shrug our shoulders as if to say: 'Manna, what is that?' (Exod. 16:15). 'For,' the Carthusian Guigo II comments, 'they had a poor and low opinion of the Word, as a contemptible thing,' just as the Jews in the New Testament found Jesus' words about the bread of His body too hard and turned away from Him. 'Nay, they turned themselves about and yearned after the fleshpots of Egypt, for they did not yet know the taste that the manna concealed within it, nor had they as yet enjoyed it.' It is of little use to hear the Word in a superficial way; we must really attend to it, assimilate it eagerly and nurture it in our heart. Of the manna that is God's Word we can never have enough. 'The man who had gathered more had not too much, the man who had gathered less had not too little. Each found he had gathered what he needed' (Exod. 16:18). God who is greater than our heart adapts Himself to each one of us. Every believer gets the Word that he needs—and in such measure that he can absorb and assimilate it. But this demands of him a lot of effort, practice and ascetic discipline. Guigo exhorts us: 'Gather up, gather up the manna and grind it at the mill. Such toiling is hard, but rich in rewards. For of the harvest of your hands shall you eat, blessed are you, prosperity will be yours' (Ps. 128:2). Grind with the mill of the body and of the soul, and you shall find the kernel. Grind the body with fasting, working and keeping watch; and the soul by attentive reading of the divine Law (this is Holy Writ). Do not let this Law forsake your heart: repeat it (meditari), mutter it (meditari) over and over again; nose it out, time after time, and you will come to understand the taste of the manna (the Word). Witness the words of him who said: 'How sweet are your words, O Lord, they are sweeter to my throat than honey and the honey dripping from the comb' (Ps. 19:10; 119:103).[4]

Keeping watch about the Word

Now that Word and heart have found each other they must try to stay together and so to persevere. This calls for great vigilance. Now that for the first time the heart is really operative, it will try to remain always in movement. And we ourselves will have to see to it that our heart remains our dwelling-place. That will not be easy; for we are always having to let go of our heart and be distracted, when out of sheer necessity we have other things to do or make use of our discursive reason, of our imagination, and so on. So long as these other faculties are not in complete harmony with our heart and have not yet been drenched, as it were, in the heart's superabundance; so long as they have not been assimilated and geared in to the heart's peculiar rhythm, there will be a danger that we loose our hold on Word and heart and that our heart will go back to sleep.

But anyone determined to persist in prayer must apply himself to this interior vigil. As the Fathers put it, he must mount guard over his heart. He must be frugal and austere in his inclinations, desires and feelings and never relax his attention. Above all he must attain to quietness, to deep, unfathomable silence. One of the Fathers observes that the person whose life is filled with much business and many cares and inwardly or outwardly is in a state of uproar is like a flask with water in it that is murky because the flask has been shaken about too much. 'If the flask is left standing for a little while, the scum sinks to the bottom and the water becomes clear and transparent. In a similar way our heart, once it is restful and steeped in profound silence, can reflect God.'[5]

Contemplation of the Word of God is bound up inseparably with silence. For the Word proceeds from the profound silence of the Holy Trinity, the 'Trinity that is the Friend of Silence' (Trinitas amica silentii), as the twelfth-century Cistercian, Adam of Perseigne, has it.[6] One Word was enough to reveal to us the deepest secret of life. In the mystery of Christmas, especially, we commemorate the silence maintained by the Word made flesh, who even before Pilate gave a demonstration of silence. Even on the cross Jesus opened His mouth only to fulfil the Scriptures. 'There is nothing that encourages to silence so powerfully and with so much authority, nothing puts so big a bridle of fear upon the restless tongue and the raging word, as the silent Word of God among men.'[7] On the one hand meditation on the Word must go hand in hand with silence. But on the other, a dead silence is senseless, unless it is filled with the Word. 'The silence without the meditation is death, like someone being buried alive,' a monk of the eleventh century observes, 'the meditation without the silence is a waste and sheer agitation. But if in the spiritual life the two go together, they induce in the soul a great silence and perfect contemplation.'[8] Outward and inward silence will little by little affect each other. Exterior silence, if practised properly, will lead to the interior sort. Getting control of the tongue may often involve a long struggle. But once mastery of the tongue has led to silence of the heart, that will in turn find expression in a state of physical silence.

'Silence,' said Isaac the Syrian, 'is the language of the angels' and 'the secret of the world to come,'[9] but silence is also the language and the secret of our heart, when it keeps a diffident watch, looking forward to the great event of salvation that will be enacted in it. Silence is a putting aside, a renouncing of all schemes, desires, inclinations and thoughts which cannot be incorporated in the aching prayer of the Spirit within us. Everything in us still affected by ambition, selfishness, sensuality, anxiety, and which prevents us from

43

expressing ourselves wholly before God. We must beware of the strange and confused world inside us with which we so readily identify. Some of the Fathers say that to every desire arising within us we must dispatch a sentinel to put the question: 'Who are you, where do you come from, which side are you on?' They mean that each and every desire must be subjected to a crisis, a judgment.

We must eventually learn to live in a degree of penury as regards our aspirations and ideas. For silence will leave a void inside us. But that void in our heart is a pit which has to be further and further excavated till we strike the water of the Spirit, bubbling up from the bottom of our heart.

One of the early Fathers said: 'A heart is like a pond. Dig deeper into the pond and the water gets clearer and clearer. Toss in dung, and it gets fouled up.'[10] Silence is a way of scooping out that void within us, of burrowing down to increase the draught. New space must be made available, where we can pierce through to the source of our being. That source is the Spirit in us, and also the Word of God. We are born of that water and of that Spirit, of this water and of this Word. The new life bubbles up in us like water; and all at once it fills to the brim the space which the silence has made available.

Once the water has found its bed within our heart, further use of the spade becomes unnecessary. True interior silence and true prayer sometimes make maintaining an outward silence less needful. For running water will itself go on scooping out its bed. 'To pray is to be a bed for the stream,' a well-known Flemish poetess once wrote. The person who has hollowed out this void within him becomes at once fully charged with inner experience of the Spirit. In his heart will flow the waters of silence, the waters of Shiloah that flow only in tranquillity (Isa. 8:6), the spring welling up to eternal life (John 4:14).

Wrestling with the Word

Vigilance goes hand in hand with a tough and difficult struggle. 'What is the hardest task of the monk?' enquired the brothers, of Prior Agathon. And he replied: 'The monk's hardest task, as I see it, is prayer. With every other disciplinary practice the monk undertakes, even if it give him much trouble and require much patience, at some point or other he will attain a measure of tranquillity; but prayer will demand of him a hard battle, up to the very end.'[11] Anyone called to penetrate to the Spirit in his heart is inevitably and inexorably confronted with evil and with the Evil One in person. Prior Evagrius, the great instructor in prayer from the desert of Scete, describes this battle as follows: 'When courage fails you, then pray. Pray in fear and trembling; pray with fervour, with sobriety, with vigilance. Take heed of the invisible enemies who are bent on evil and especially in the hour of prayer lie in wait to take us in their snares.'[12]

Whoever lets the prayer of the Spirit come to the surface of his heart is immediately confronted with a choice which for the time being others do not have to make. He must assent to prayer or give it up. This is a choice between death and life, between Spirit and flesh, between the Will of God and our own puny wills, between the immeasurable Love of the Father and our little bounded desires. Yet in that battle we have the Spirit on our side, and also the Word of God and the almighty Name of Jesus. At the same time, however, we still bear in our heart the traces of sin. And in order to depart from sin we must cling more and more closely to Jesus within us. In our ordinary, everyday life that choice is not so crucial; for it happens on the outer verge of things and of ourselves. It is partial and provisional. But in prayer that same choice occurs at the level of the *heart*, at the root of things and of us. There it would seem to become a cosmic battle, where we are the stakes in a contest between good and evil, Jesus and Satan, heaven and earth.

The man who does battle in his prayer is armed with the Word of God and the Name of Jesus. He must hurl that Name, the Fathers tell us, at the devil's head. That Name will cause the devils to vanish like dust before the wind.[13] The constant invocation of Jesus will gradually become the strongest weapon against the enemy and against temptation. For prayer is itself the weapon in its own fight.

That battle of prayer brings its own temptations: aridity and discouragement. And despite everything one has to persevere in prayer and in the Word. The spring is sometimes slow in appearing, the light tarries and our heart seems to doze off again. Then love teaches us to be patient in vigilance. Love teaches us to crane forward eagerly to, and yet be content with, the scanty food apportioned to us; love teaches perseverance. It will then be a case of prayer in the night-time and without light, of clinging hard to God in the teeth of what men call hope: a prayer of faith that is no bigger than a grain of mustard-seed but big enough to enable God to once again perform His marvellous acts. A sort of 'cock-eyed' praying in which grace operates in us invisibly but most potently and the bottom of our heart is imperceptibly, but quite certainly dug out and deepened.

This is the most difficult ascesis, which has to be fought out behind the scenes, as it were, and purifies us from within, more and better than any physical discipline would do, even though the body too, must gradually be drawn into this ascesis.

Thus an interaction develops between ascesis and prayer. Is it a case of the ascetic discipline being exercised in the hope of our finding the path to prayer? Or is it the condition of prayer that causes us to die to sin? In other words: is it dying to sin that activates prayer within us? Or conversely, is it the current of prayer that washes away the traces of sin from our heart? The man to whom God has given the task of praying can no longer answer that question. It is enough for him that he is experiencing new life, that his heart has become wide awake, alive and kicking, that he is listening and talking to God in his heart. For this life he has given up everything. To this life in himself he is totally committed. This has now become his sole task; his life's work. Actually, it is no longer his own work, it is God's work in him, *Opus Dei*, in the primitive sense of the term.

'Rocking and chewing' the Word

Word and heart have now grown together, as it were. The Bible has a richly variegated vocabulary to draw upon for expressing how the Word of God engrosses the human heart, and how the heart as it were appropriates the Word and, having itself become Word of God, is in its turn enabled to utter and interpret the fulness of God's Word, before men in proclamation, before God in prayer and praise and eucharist and thanksgiving.

The heart takes in the Word, consumes it and digests it (Ezek. 3:1–3). A man will harbour the Word in his heart (Ps. 119:11), cherish it in his breast (Job 23:12), cling to it (Luke 8:15), embrace it and stick to it (Acts 16:14), toss it to and fro in his heart (Luke 2:19), murmur it day and night (Ps. 1:2). And finally, a man will come to dwell in the Word as in his own home, just as the Word too, dwells in us and makes us its home (Col. 3:16). The Word of God and the heart of man are at home with each other. The more frequently and powerfully the Word makes itself heard, the longer our heart will keep its vigil and stay awake. And the more alertly and attentively our heart listens to the Word, the deeper it penetrates into the mysteries of the Spirit. Our heart is fed more and more by the Word of God. The stronger that enables the heart to become, the more the Word of God is going to illuminate, the clearer and more copious it will be for whoever listens to it.

The ancient texts refer to this interior confrontation between Word and heart as *meditatio*—not meditation, that is, consideration or reflection in our more rational sense of the word, but in the primitive sense of a constant repetition, a persistent murmuring of the same words. Cassian calls this the *volutatio cordis* (Col. 10:13), the rocking of the heart, which rises and falls like a ship, dipping in the swell of the Spirit; and so the heart tumbles and turns the Word of God to and fro within it in order gradually to make it its own. For this people in the Middle Ages used a surprising but very suggestive metaphor: *ruminari*—the *chewing* of the Word. One cannot help thinking of some sleepy cows, settled down in the shade of a tree somewhere, peacefully and incessantly chewing the cud.

The picture is a bit crude, but very vivid: it speaks to us of tranquillity, of being totally engrossed, of patiently digesting things.

This is again an important element in the prelude to prayer. The Word that I am turning over in my heart is, after all, no merely human word without life or lustre. It is God's Word; that is to say, it is a seed of life that can strike root and germinate; it is a glowing coal that purifies and gives warmth; a spark that can set my heart ablaze like a dry haystack.

Of course, we must again take good care at this point not to wander off into an intellectual analysis of some truth or other concerning God. At this moment any attempt at rational thinking would not only serve as a distraction but would be a death-blow to the new life that was on the point of being born. The fact is that we are standing here at the very base, the very springs of our heart and of our existence, with our defences down, exposed to the love of God, to the power of the Spirit and to the consuming omnipotence of his Word.

What is actually happening? In the course of listening to God's Word, either at public service in church or in my private reading, I have suddenly been struck by a particular saying. My heart has been wounded, punctured—literally: *compunctus*—by this Word. And now I cannot cast this Word off any more. It gives me pause. I dwell upon it, stand guard over it. I take it over and repeat it slowly in the silence of my heart, I *rock* it to and fro in this interior region of myself, I *ruminate* upon it, *chew it over*, I let it soak right into my heart. It amounts, quite literally, to a *flushing out* of the heart.

What every biblical utterance may achieve in our heart is true in the first place of the Word par excellence, the summation of every saying in the Bible, the Name above every name, the Name of Jesus. The patient repetition of that Name within the heart is called the Jesus-prayer. But the structure in this case is the same. The Name of Jesus makes our heart wide awake and, conversely, constantly calling upon Jesus helps us to discover his presence and make it more and more real. 'Consequently,' an ancient author says, 'vigilance and the Jesus-prayer invariably go together. They support and complement each other. Attentiveness helps to promote continuing prayer, and that in its turn fosters vigilance and attentiveness.'[14]

The following anecdote has come down to us from the age of the very earliest monks: 'A brother put the question to Prior Macarius: "Which of the monk's tasks is the most pleasing to God?" Macarius replied: "Happy he who perseveres in the blessed Name of our Lord Jesus Christ, and does so without ceasing and with a broken heart. The monastic life knows no labour more pleasing to God. One should keep chewing this blessed food, like a sheep that returns its food to the mouth, chewing it again and tasting the sweetness of it till the food, now finely ground, drops down to the inmost places of the heart, thence to spread its sweetness and its richness in belly and bowels. Behold what a youthful bloom there is upon the cheeks of the sheep, thanks to the sweetness of that which he has chewed and chewed again with his mouth. May our Lord Jesus Christ give us the grace of his sweet and fecund Name." [15] To this Jesus-prayer we shall return later on in the book.

The superabundance of the heart

We stand now on the threshold of prayer. Our heart has been awakened. It sees Jesus, it hears His voice, it rejoices in His Word. That Word has been turned over and over in our heart. It has purified us, cleansed us, and we have grown familiar with it. Perhaps we are even beginning to resemble this Word. Now too, it can take root in our heart and bear fruit. Now it may even become the Word of God in our flesh.

So long as we ourselves were still intent on the Word of God in our heart, we had come no further than the prelude. There comes a moment when we yield up God's Word to the Spirit within us. Then it is that our heart gives birth to prayer. And then at last the Word of God has become truly ours. We have then discovered and realized our most profound, our true identity. And then the Name of Jesus has become our name also. And together with Jesus we may with one voice call God: Abba, Father!

Prayer is the superabundance of the heart. It is brim-full and running over with love and praise, as once it was with Mary, when the Word took root in her body. So too, our heart breaks out into a Magnificat. Now the Word has achieved its 'glorious course' (2 Thess. 3:1): it has gone out from God and been sown in the good soil of the heart. Having now been *chewed over* and assimilated, it is regenerated in the heart, to the praise of God. It has taken root in us and is now bearing its fruit: we in our turn utter the Word and send it back to God. We have become Word; we are prayer. Thus prayer is the precious fruit of the Word—Word of God that has become wholly our own and in that way has been inscribed deep in our body and our psyche, and that now can become our response to the Love of the Father. The Spirit stammers it out in our heart, without our doing anything about it. It bubbles up, it flows, it runs like living water. It is no longer we who pray, but the prayer prays itself in us. The divine life of the risen Christ ripples softly in our heart.

The slow work of transfiguring the cosmos has had a beginning in us. The whole creation has been waiting for this moment: the revelation of the glory of the children of God (Rom. 8:19). It is going on in secret and quite unpretentiously; and yet already in Spirit and truth. We are still in the world, and we dwell already with Jesus near the Father. We still live in the flesh, and the Spirit has already made us wholly captive. For the veil has fallen from our heart, and with unveiled faces we reflect like mirrors the glory and brightness of Jesus, as we ourselves are being recreated in His image, from glory to glory, by His Spirit (2 Cor. 3:18).

So the Word of Christ resides in our heart, in all its richness (Col. 3:16). In it we are rooted, on it we are founded, by it we order our conduct in life, and all the time we overflow with praise and thanksgiving (Col. 2:6-7). This eucharist-thanksgiving has now become our life (Col. 3:15), the superabundance of our heart, the liturgy of the new world that deep within us we already celebrate. We are in fact temples of the Spirit (1 Cor. 6:19).

THE PSALM AS RESPONSE

The process described in the foregoing chapter, carried on as it is between heart and Word, for a long time bore its fruit in the psalms. That may best be illustrated in a chapter devoted to examining how the psalms arose and have been used in prayer. We shall also attempt to answer the question—a difficult one in these days—as to how the psalms can still be used in praying now.

Ever since the time of the primitive Church the psalms have had a privileged place in the prayer-life of the faithful, whether the prayer has been liturgical or private. When they were inherited by Christianity from Judaism, the psalms brought their popularity with them and kept it over many centuries. That transfer raised no problems.

We still have the psalms in the revised breviary; and as always, they occupy an important place in it. Their favoured position, however, no longer goes unchallenged. Many people have difficulty when it comes to using the psalms as prayer. So much so, in fact, that a justifiable use of them in such a context is for some the most acute problem presented by the modern version of the office.

It is fair to say that there exists something of a crisis in this regard. The crisis became inevitable as soon as we began to have trouble in sensing the spiritual efficacy of the text of the psalms. As long as we were still reciting them in Latin, this was not immediately evident to us. Behind the screen provided by a dead language a great many things could be discreetly concealed, while the unrelenting ritualism that marked every celebration lulled all and sundry to sleep.

With the switch to the vernacular this curtain was lifted and the psalm abruptly shaken out of its slumbers. Partly, at any rate, in the more or less unabashed coarseness of its very human language, the psalm has confronted us in a new guise; and it is the unexpected novelty of it that gives offence. The language fails to impress, the images sound outlandish or quaint, the sentiments are so crude and uncivilized. There is no reference to the Church, very little about the Spirit, nothing about Jesus and His resurrection. To feel at home again with the use of the psalms in prayer it is not enough to adapt the text, in image and vocabulary, to modern norms. Although that is much to be desired, it does not get beyond a superficial tidying up and touching up of the Word in its external aspect. We are still caught up in the trappings of the letter; and the penalty is to let slip the vital breath, the *pneuma*, of the Word.

We are still working away at the shell, while the kernel stays out of reach.

A living word

Every word of men is a living word. Even the humblest word uttered by a human being is born of a vital experience and is permeated with the vital breath of the speaker. It is for that reason elastic and supple. The same word can express various shades of meaning and address us at several different levels. In the language of ordinary conversation, and especially in that of science, any given word conveys a single, limited and well-defined meaning. But of itself every word is in the nature of things 'unfathomable'. It has a dimension of depth that can only be explored and put across in a gradual process.

In most cases, however, these hidden depths do not matter very much. Indeed, where clarity is concerned it is better that a word's unconscious undertones be heard as little as possible. But in other instances, exactly the opposite is true: the word should be apprehended in all its richness. It performs its duty—one might say, its calling—only when it takes us by surprise, with all its nuances, conscious and unconscious. The listener must be invested by the word from tip to toe, must be stirred and challenged at every level of his being as a man.

Above all is this the case with poetry. It is in poetry that a word, any word, fully attains to its life and power, is charged to bursting point with the living breath of some human experience to which it testifies and which it conveys to others. We have to remember that what is involved here is much more than the business of interpreting and assimilating ideas. The word, after all, is *pregnant* with life, is capable of begetting new life in anyone able to listen to it in silent surrender.

The poet is actually *poiētēs*, in the etymological sense of the term: *maker, creator*. He is proximate to the Creator Himself. God created through His Word. Each and every poet is called, in the full *potency* of each human word, to complete God's creation in the things he celebrates or in the people for whom he does it. Because every human word has something to do with the word of creation, no poem is very far from prayer. Thus every word has a calling to become prayer. 'I would like to love words so deeply that each one became for me a prayer'—'Je voudrais aimer si profondément les mots que chacun me devînt une prière' (Pierre Emmanuel). The last and ripest fruit of a word, far exceeding any poem, is ultimately a prayer.

A word of men

The word uttered as 'psalm' in the first place matured within the heart of a man and was born on human lips. The feelings it evokes are not alien to us, although the imagery in which it is expressed is sometimes no longer immediately understandable. Yet it is the human being who is revealed in this as in every poem, the human who transcends race, frontier and period, the eternal human slumbering in our heart, whom only gradually, and then only in part, we allow to mount into our consciousness.

Here, partly at least, lies the mysterious force of the psalms as poetry that grips each individual with such impetuosity. It not only speaks to the human being brought to consciousness in us, but may also move a man at the level of the unconscious, not yet assimilated regions of his deeper personality, where he expresses himself towards his fellows and towards God without inhibition or bias but also unawares. Everything that the psalm touches and brings to life within us, however, we cannot accept just like that. The psalmist was a human being hurt by sin who shouted out his sorrow and distraction before God. His is a catalogue of fear, despair, rage, hatred; and he is evidently not inclined to hide these emotions. Not everyone reading the psalms twenty centuries later realizes that all this is still lurking in his heart. The more he identifies with the received norms of the group in which he lives—even though the norms may be those of the Gospel—the more difficult it is for him to dare to recognize himself in these heathen emotions. The more infrequently he has succeeded in admitting himself really and truly a sinner confronted with the grace of God, the more insupportably will these all too human words burn upon his lips.

The feeling of oddness that assails the modern reader when using some of the psalms as prayer arises partly at this level. Because each group has its own taboos, and those taboos are always shifting, there will also be a shift taking place in the strength of feeling evinced against this or that by the average psalm-praying person.

It may be asked at this point whether it is psychologically healthy for someone to suppress such feelings in his heart and consequently eliminate their expression from the psalms. The human tension and the inner dynamic given an outlet through these feelings in the psalms ought not perhaps to be lost. Might they not be better orientated and turn out in the end to be of benefit to someone who is all the time growing and developing on positive lines? Admittedly, they do in the first place reveal the sinful person whom everyone recognizes in himself and with whom he must come to terms. But as soon as that reconciliation has been achieved, with the person himself and between the person and God, may not the dynamic of those feelings then be given a new twist and directed into positive channels? If so, the words of the ancient psalms, which at one time were an outlet for quite primitive emotions, may perhaps grow along with a person and trace the process as life develops within him.

On the other hand, what the human poet comes out with in the psalm is not the final word of that psalm; and the breath of life with which it is imbued is not of this world alone.

A Word of God

In their naked and literal human aspect the psalms are at once poetry and prayer: prayer indeed, but in a poetic form. Their potency, however, is not a merely human thing. God is Himself using and producing the word that they address to man. That word is instinct, not only with the living breath of a human individual—albeit that of a creator-poet—but also with the breath of God, who is creator-Spirit. The experience which the words of the psalm interpret and convey is ultimately the experience which God Himself creates in hearts that listen to Him and are open to Him.

More, therefore, than any word of man and any of man's poetry the Word of God is fathomless and inexhaustible. Anyone who tries to encompass it can only constrict it to what he himself is capable of assimilating; for the Word of God towers high above what man today can understand of it. It has a life and history all its own. Every Word of God can be measured only by the fulness of time. It never ceases to accompany the Love of God for the world and to realize and validate that Love again and again.

The import of this Word, therefore, cannot be settled once for all. It is bounding with life and engenders life in anyone who will attend to it. In His Word God is continuously at His work of creation. In every liturgy He is building His Church, which He calls together around the Word. In each and every believer with heart and spirit open to the Word, He burrows out unsuspected depths, an abyss of knowledge and of love.

In this process the psalms have a special place. In the inspired Scriptures God utters His Word to man. With the psalms it is just the other way round. Here God puts into the mouth of man the Word that man is to offer Him in response. These are no strange or novel words, however. They turn out, on closer inspection, to be the utterances of the Bible itself—but elevated into poetry and prayer. Just as the Bible contains historical books, so too are there historical psalms: wisdom-books and wisdom psalms, prophetic books and prophetic psalms. You will find the entire Bible in the psalms—but find it in the guise of poetry and prayer. In the words of the psalms the Bible reaches a peak of vital relevancy and creative *power*. Prior Philemon, whose *Logos askitikos* has been preserved in the *Philokalia* (1, 241–252), was asked why he so much relished the book of psalms, more than any other part of Scripture. He replied: 'I assure you that God has instilled the power of the psalms in my poor heart, as happened with the prophet David. Without their sweetness I could not any longer live, nor yet without the immensity of meditation they enshrine. For the psalms contain all of Holy Writ.'

The psalms indeed contain all of Holy Writ—but not simply in the form of a résumé; rather as man's living response to the Word of God. A response that comes not only from man but is engendered in his heart by God's Word itself.

The 'glorious course' of the Word (2 Thess. 3:1)

In the previous chapter we were describing how the Word completes its cycle between God and the listening heart of man. The special place of the psalm in this 'glorious course' is immediately obvious; for the psalm comes into being at the very instant when the heart of the attentive believer, having taken in the Word of God, utters that Word anew in the guise of prayer. This process occurs not at the level of the intellect but at the far deeper level of the heart, where we are able to listen to God and approach Him with the core of our personality.

'In the heart' the Word is listened to, is received, appropriated. There it will be born as psalm and as prayer. From the Word prayed there in the heart of a man the psalm emerges. The word it speaks is a Word of God, which from the very outset was charged already with God's Spirit and so was sent forth into a human being. It is heard and received by that man's spirit, to be replenished and enriched through a new experience of faith in dialogue between spirit and Spirit. In that way it can once more be interpreted to God by a human heart and return at last to Him in praise and thanksgiving. More than ever, therefore, the psalm is Word of God and word of man, a superabundance of the Word and of the heart: a place of love, where the Spirit of God and the spirit of man come closest together. The point of contact between the two is the interior prayer, the mutual dialogue between God and man, the silent liturgy celebrated without pause in every human heart. The standard and principal formulation of this interior liturgy we find in the psalms.

In the Old Testament it was this process that gave birth to the psalms. It had its consummation in Jesus Christ, Word of God made man, cornerstone of the two testaments and of the Bible. Jesus took from the psalms in making his own prayer. .In his death and resurrection, and presently in his return, the psalms attain their deepest import. Up to Jesus they had been only a summary of the Old Testament. In Jesus they are turned from water into wine, pass over from the letter to the spirit. Since Him, they celebrate also the good news, from gospel to apocalypse. The risen Lord is for ever the one and only psalmist, ceaselessly living and praying, above before the face of His Father, here below in every liturgy celebrated by His Church.

In the Lord Jesus the word of man is always the Word of God. What He preaches, tallies with what He sings; what He performs, with what He prays. He is Himself pre-eminently the living Word, and for that reason too, the psalm that never ceases, is never prayed out. All the human emotions that come to the top in the psalm, therefore, already have their completion in Jesus. Sorrow never goes unaccompanied by joy, sin and contrition have already found forgiveness, despair is the first step to faith and trust, hate is the bad side of a great love, eros points to the irresistible nature of agapē, death of itself proclaims life. This does not mean that the thoroughly human side of these emotions is thrust away or disregarded. On the contrary, they become deeper and more real. The Spirit releases them from the chaos of the letter and of the flesh. In Jesus they recover the deepest root of their dynamism, because they then coincide with the Word of God which is their own word of creation. They speak now of nothing but the coming of God's Kingdom and of the marvellous power and the signs that go with it.

The Spirit in which Jesus prayed and re-created the psalms is poured out on every baptized person, who in the same Spirit can now, like Jesus, make the psalm his own and pray it anew. For him too, its ancient words will come alive and be fulfilled in him. All the time the Word is acquiring new dimensions. In the Spirit it is deepened in every aspect and direction, so that every tone and undertone of this Word vibrates in harmony. That is why it is of necessity a poetic word, although the ultimate dimensions of the Word far transcend the potentialities of all created poetry. For it is measured and gauged not just by the *pneuma*, by the vital breath of a puny and limited human being, but by the *Pneuma* of God Himself, which creates and impels all life, and is everywhere bringing the process of salvation to its completion.

Never again, therefore, can the psalm be read, still less prayed, 'according to the letter'; for a psalm prayed in *that* way would be in the strictest sense a contradiction in terms. The truth is that a psalm can only be a psalm—as distinct from an archaeological document—to the degree that it *is alive*, that is to say, is prayed anew in our heart by the Spirit.

Word and Spirit

The praying of a psalm can only be done *pneumatikōs*, which is to say, *in the Spirit*. What any psalm means, therefore, will depend on the Spirit in which it is read or prayed. Like every Word of God, each psalm too, has a life of its own. It begins as a tiny seed, germinates, shoots up and expands. In itself its future knows no bounds. In the Old Testament what the psalm celebrated was a mere foreshadowing of the Kingdom of God. By means of the same psalm Jesus talks of the Kingdom which is already present in Him. The Holy Spirit uses it today in the Church to maintain expectancy. The Word will be exhausted only when God is all in all. Thus the psalm has a close bearing on the whole process of salvation, from the first Adam, via the coming of Jesus, the second Adam, up to His return at the close of the Age. Because the Word is imbued with God's *Pneuma*, it is more and more, and better and better able to signalize that growing thing which is the People of God *en route*, on their journey. In the rhythm of the Spirit each and every Word grows along with salvation–history in its forward progress.

This happened for the first time—a crucial and definitive occasion—in the prayer of Jesus. The very same process is carried forward daily through the believer who takes the Word into himself and utters it again in his singing of the psalm. For someone who lives by Jesus and the Spirit little or not at all, the psalm will be dead or will just be part of the Old Testament. He will be unable to get beyond the letter, raw and human as it is. But for anyone who lives by the Spirit imparted to us by Jesus, the psalm too will live. And if anyone is growing in the same Spirit, the psalm will grow with him. For him new vistas will always be appearing on the horizon of the Word. The limits are distended and burst open. Jesus and His Kingdom are already close to that man.

We need not be afraid, therefore, of ever becoming too familiar with the psalms. They can never bore us, provided we are always growing with their intrinsic dynamism, that is, with the Spirit who inspires the psalms and keeps them alive. This assumes that we are progressively laying ourselves open to the Spirit and yielding ourselves to Him. As our outward man decreases from day to day while our inner man grows, so the letter of the psalm too falls away like a shell that has become superfluous, whereas the essential content of *Pneuma*, the *spiritual potency* of the psalm is more and more plainly felt. The two processes are correlative, the one depending on the other and operating on it. The man who lives 'after the flesh' and by the works of the flesh kills the Spirit within him and will likewise find in the psalm nothing but the flesh and will stay trapped within the letter of its human words. The man who lives in the Spirit will also discover the Spirit in the psalms, without effort or constraint, above and beyond the artificial acrobatics of this or that pointed application.

From spirit to Spirit

From our prayer grounded in the psalms we may deduce the condition of our heart. The psalm is as it were the barometer of our life in the Spirit and of our prayer; for psalm and heart are each in their own way a *place* of prayer, the soil out of which it grows to full flower. Psalms can only be prayed 'with the heart' (Eph. 5:19); and the heart in its turn is fertilized and fed by the psalm in the activity of prayer. The psalm is at once the fruit of prayer and its new seed.

Perhaps we can now take stock of the tragic misunderstanding springing up between the psalms and the modern Christian at prayer. The use of God's Word as prayer presupposes a whole anthropology; and this is true of every form of prayer. Prayer is, after all, a 'lived', existential anthropology: it has to do with the person who is gradually being captivated by the Spirit, heart and body, and so is being transformed from spirit to Spirit, into the image of God in Jesus Christ.

If we merely approach the psalms with a particular feeling and a particular logic so as to extract religious experience from them—which then still has to be verified in accordance with current norms—we are giving the psalm's own life and *potency* no chance at all.

We have to risk exposing ourselves, in all our humanity, to the psalm's dynamism, so as to make our surrender to the *pneuma* of the psalm. This *pneuma* is in the first place that of the poet who qua human being composed the psalm. The spirit of a man knows what goes on in the human heart, boring through to the deepest foundation of every human experience. That is why the psalm does not even spare the sin that is in us. It exposes the lot: desolation, fear, rancour, vindictiveness.

By so doing the psalm brings us much closer to our real condition as human beings—but only so that at this sinful level we may be rescued by God's Spirit. For the *pneuma* of the psalm is also the divine *Pneuma*; and the human words are there only so that, being inspired, they may become the Word of God. At the same time, therefore, the psalm takes us to the ultimate depths of the heart of God. It lays God bare for us in Jesus: love, mercy, almightiness, triumph. All this assumes that as Paul put it, we 'being filled with the Spirit, go on praying the psalms in our hearts' (Eph. 5:18–19), listening, that is, with attention, receiving with patience, persistently, lovingly murmuring the psalms, being assimilated as it were by the psalm itself, to the rhythm of our own spirit, beginning to thrill in harmony with the spirit of the psalmist and with the Spirit of God Himself.

For the man of today with his scientific training it is not all that easy to make himself at home with this *spiritual* technique—or *technique in the Spirit*. He is used to standing off from the text, treating it as an object for discussion or examination. But it is even less easy to accept the spiritual *truth*, the reality with which each of us personally is presented in the psalm: first the relative character of our human emotions, so hard for us to accept; then the lofty demands of the Spirit that keep pressing themselves upon us, as they arise out of the psalm, by way of our own heart and our own lips.

Yet the one *pneuma* never goes without the other. The *pneuma* of man calls up the *Pneuma* of God. Man's sinfulness is there to be cleansed by the Spirit of God, and the human *pneuma* of the poet to be subsumed into the *Pneuma* of God. So in the psalm a continuing dialogue is in progress, a dialogue from spirit to Spirit; and there is growing a fruitful tension in which time and again a revelation is accomplished. That dialogue takes place in the praying heart which as it listens yields to the tension. In that way our spirit learns how great was the sin and how unutterably greater is God's Love in Jesus Christ. In every psalm, therefore, the Spirit of God testifies to our spirit that it is poured by God into our heart (Rom. 5:5), that we really are children of God (Rom. 8:16) and that God is Love (1 John 4:8).

Sixth Chapter

THE WORD MADE FLESH

'The Word was made flesh, he lived among us' (John 1 : 14). The Word that resided with the Father and the Spirit, the Word in and through whom the Father created all things, this Word the Father in His plan of salvation has caused to become a human being. The Word became one of us. In Jesus, man and God have embraced each other. God—that is, in the first place, the Father—sends forth the Son, the most precious thing a father possesses, his image, his likeness. With God's becoming man our redemption had begun. 'We human beings serve the works of the flesh,' as Paul puts it in one of his letters (Eph. 2 : 3). We were far removed from God, we were no longer at peace with God. It was hard for His Word to get through to us; and we were scarcely able to receive it. But in His unsurpassable Love, One Person of the Trinity clothed Himself in sinful flesh. Jesus is the Lamb of God that bears and takes away the sins of the world (John 1 : 29). The good Shepherd goes out to seek what was lost, the thing He loved above all else (Matt. 18 : 12). In this Love He has gone to the furthest limit, accepting even death (Phil. 2 : 8). When in the Garden of Olives He had fought His agonizing struggle to the end—His sweat falling in drops of blood to the ground—men nailed Him to the cross and He died: love to the utmost.

In the body of Christ our sinful body is nailed to the cross. In the death of Jesus, it too dies. The sin of our body is overcome and its power nullified in the flesh (Rom. 8 : 3). For the almighty power of the Father has raised Jesus from the dead, has clothed Him with a new body over which death no longer has any control (Rom. 6 : 9). His human body is now full of God's glory, permeated by the Spirit. Thanks to the Passover that one of us has undergone, our body can be reborn of the Spirit, as spirit. Now it can itself become a vehicle of the Spirit. For as our body used at one time to be a body-of-flesh, so now it can become a body-of-*pneuma*, that is a spiritual body.

Again, in our body, once invested by the Spirit, the springs of living water must well up. Just as the 'exalted' body of Jesus on the cross (John 12 : 32), in death and resurrection, becomes a well-spring of the Spirit—like the rock from which Moses struck running water for the thirsty travellers in the wilderness—so that same Spirit in our body becomes a spring always bubbling and rising to eternal life. For our body also is a dwelling-place of the Spirit and a temple of unending prayer.

So the Word of God, as we give our whole attention to it, not only fructifies our heart but thrives and flourishes also in our body —as indeed it must. In our members the Word must be made flesh. Our entire being, spirit, heart and body, must be taken up into the cycle of the Word.

Praying with a body

Our body, therefore, plays a central role in the return to the Father, with Jesus, in the Spirit. In our body the Spirit can well up and prayer must be born. But every prayer, however secret and however interior it may be, will be mirrored in the body. Prayer cannot happen without the body, either with beginners or with those who are advanced in prayer. Gradually, prayer and the Spirit take possession of the body. Body and Spirit are bound up inseparably together.

Prior Agathon said: 'Man is like a tree. The foliage stands for the toiling (*kopos*, *labor*, *podvig*) of the body, the fruit is the interior attention. For the sake of this fruit we have to apply ourselves thoroughly to the attention of the heart. We need both the protection and the strength of the leaves, that is, physical exertion.'[1] Thus ascesis and contemplation, physical and spiritual work, always go hand in hand. They appear on the same trunk, receive the vital sap of the roots that have the same nourishing soil. The fruit is more important than the foliage; and woe to the tree on which only leaves are found (Matt. 21:19). And yet the fruit will not ripen if the foliage gives no protection or nourishment, because the leaves are indispensable. The figure of speech that Prior Agathon uses here is a rich one and full of profound wisdom. We are a long way here from the neo-Platonic dichotomy, so called, at whose door, without any distinction, the whole patristic tradition has been laid often enough, and which ascribes more value to the soul than to the body. On the contrary, in man's return to God the body has a very special role. It leads man towards the state of perfection in which he will be made wholly new in the Spirit. The body is an indispensable road to prayer and to love in its fulness.

St. Anthony—the Father of all monks—shows how the Spirit takes possession simultaneously of the body and the soul, empowering and assisting both in the process of sanctification. Body and soul are like two gradients. Prayer is then the top of the mountain. On the path to prayer the body (one of the slopes) obtains the gift of watching and fasting. The ascetic's sensual passions are tranquillized and revert to the former state which God had conceived and created for them, when love alone existed and there was as yet no discord in man.. The soul (the other slope of the mountain) receives the gift of vigilance to fight the spiritual battle, assisted by the Word of Holy Scripture that heals and sanctifies. Thus the soul is enabled to recognize the body's ills and to help bring about their spiritual cure: 'The Word of God is something alive and active: it cuts like any double-edged sword but more finely: it can slip through the place where the soul is divided from the spirit, or joints from the marrow; it can judge the secret emotions and thoughts' (Heb. 4:12). In the end the whole body, in both the struggle of ascesis and the tranquillity of prayer, will become one with the Spirit in the service of prayer and love. In this every member takes its part, says Anthony, 'from the head to the feet,' eyes, ears and tongue, which now praises God (cf. James 3:2–12). A person is made altogether new 'by the power of the Spirit that gives rest to the whole body', while his hands are raised in token of prayer and open to display loving-kindness.[2]

Is this still ascesis? It may already be transfiguration, the image of God shining again in a man's countenance, a body totally involved in prayer and manifesting it quite without effort. The Fathers call this 'the resurrection prior to resurrection' or 'the minor resurrection'; and St. Anthony perceives in this already 'some degree of participation in the spiritual body we are due to receive only at the general resurrection'.

Between these two aspects of the life of prayer, exterior and interior, leaves and fruit, we should not wish to make a choice. Never should the one take precedence over the other: neither leaves over fruit or fruit over leaves. But all outward toil must blossom and bear fruit in the interior eucharist of the heart, and this inward prayer is not possible without the ascesis of the body. This constant interaction between the heart and the body, which is spoken of in the monastic writings of all periods, is *the* typical feature of the technique of Christian prayer. A whole anthropology, a distinctive insight into the structure of man underlies it. The idea is certainly not that the physical is to make way for the spiritual, and the material for the immaterial. In that case prayer would simply cut the body right out—and man with it. On the contrary, by way of grace and prayer the body returns to its original state. It is no longer a 'body of sin' (Rom. 6:6) or a 'body of humiliation' (Phil. 2:8), a symbol of contrariety with God and with other men, the locus of an unremitting struggle that can only issue in death and annihilation. From being a *body-of-death* it becomes the *body-of-life*, the moment it ceases to be governed by sin and the seeds of perdition it carried with it. On the contrary, the body is then able to yield itself completely to the Spirit, to let itself be taken over little by little by His power and the new life in Jesus.

This is a lifelong process of watching and prayer, in which the ascesis of the body and the unceasing concentration of the heart on God are bound up inseparably with each other. It is here that besides his heart, man's body too must play a crucial role. After all, this is the terrain where up to now sin has been in control and where its influence has to be nullified by the power of the Holy Spirit. Just as Jesus did in death and resurrection, so too must the Christian 'defeat sin in his body' (Rom. 8:3). That he cannot manage by himself; it is the Easter power of Jesus that does it. In his body every Christian is handed over as it were to two conflicting powers that mean to capture him. The body is the arena in which they unleash their mutual hostility. Thus the Christian's body is a battleground for sin and Jesus or, as Paul puts it, for the struggle between the flesh and the Spirit. But as the Christian carries sin within him, so too he bears the seed of grace, deposited in his body at baptism. He has been incorporated into the death of Jesus and clothed with the power of His resurrection.

Between baptism and dying that marvellous power, that strength, is to unfold in him more and more. The sacramental sign must now become reality itself, permeating the whole of life to the point of visible death, reality in deadly seriousness, reality writ in blood. 'Give your blood and get the Spirit,' said one of the early Fathers.[3] Each person baptized undergoes the death of Jesus in his body, so that the power of his resurrection may become more and more evident in the same body (Phil. 3:10–11). Indeed, to the extent that he concretely dies to sin, the resurrection life begins to flower and bear fruit in his body.

The same dynamic is at work in prayer, as in ascesis. It is the finest fruit, and also the most essential, of the Easter energy with which the world and man have been charged by the resurrection of Jesus. So for the monk it can always be Easter,[4] just as it is also always Lent.[5] Of the new man, born of the Passover of Jesus, prayer is the keystone, as it were. For like death, and even above and beyond death, praying is 'love to the utmost' (John 13:1). Prayer is this anthropology-in-action. In it man is able to reach his complete and supreme fulfilment. Only prayer can express in words the depths of man, hold the key to his mystery. Man creates with his prayer the place and the moment at which, in a body, sinful flesh passes over to the Spirit of God. This is the Passover of Jesus, renewed in man; the Spirit that is poured out upon the flesh; the crown set upon the work of Jesus and the Father.

The classic elements of the technique of Christian prayer, we shall now discuss, one by one, in greater detail. They are: celibacy, solitude and silence, watching and fasting. In most experiential encounters with prayer these have recurred over twenty centuries, from the New Testament writings up to the modern mystics. We find them in non-Christian mysticism as well. It seems likely, therefore, that these techniques constitute a sort of basis on which man's practice of prayer can easily develop. We shall be considering this natural orientation of each technique in our analysis; but we shall not leave it at that. Actually, in Christian prayer these techniques are made to serve a process of interior growth in which the driving force and direction come entirely from the Holy Spirit. Thus the natural tendency of each technique to be conducive to prayer is channelled as it were on to the spiritual level within us and is focused upon the Paschal mystery of Jesus. It has to become a sign and expression of our dying with Jesus and our rising again with Him. No wonder; for Jesus was Himself unmarried, He preferred to go in search of solitude, He spent many a night in prayer and finally He endured forty days of fasting in the desert.

Celibacy and prayer

When Paul says that anyone who is joined to the Lord is one spirit with Him (1 Cor. 6:17), this is in the context a reference to the purity of the body. Celibacy, virginity, is meant to be in the service of prayer; and the same is true of temporary abstention from sexual intercourse within marriage. 'Do not refuse each other except by mutual consent, and then only for an agreed time, to leave yourselves free for prayer; then come together again' (1 Cor. 7:5). For even in a person's sexual life there is concealed a dynamic that has to be released for the benefit of the Spirit and of prayer.

Man and woman are indeed, according to the Bible, created in the image of God (Gen. 1:27). This in their specific being-as-man and being-as-woman. The man is the image of God in his masculinity. He reflects the Love of God in so far as that is strength, stalwartness and fidelity. The Bible expresses that aspect of God's love with the word *emeth, veritas*, truth and faithfulness. The man is the image of the *veritas* of the Creator.

The woman too, in her femininity, is an image of God's love. But she reflects more its goodness, its tenderness. She is an image of God's solicitude: *hesed, misericordia.*

God is both together, *misericordia et veritas*, mercy and fidelity. He is so in a single nature in which the power of His graciousness and that of His strength coincide in a manner beyond our understanding. To our way of feeling, tenderness and toughness are opposites. This results from the fact that we can only know the love of God in terms of the duality of the human sexes into which it is as it were bifurcated.

For since God represents Himself in man, He requires a twofold image, the one aspect complementing the other: man and woman, father and mother. The fulness of God's Love is normally portrayed and lived out in the two together. Though woman cannot do without man, says Paul, neither can man do without woman, in the Lord (1 Cor. 11:11). So as to reflect on the one side God's mighty Love and on the other His solicitous concern, it is necessary for man and woman to come together and be fruitful on earth as God is fruitful, is fertile in His Love.

In the solitariness of their own sex man and woman are incomplete. Although unconscious of it, they carry in their heart the other part of God's image. Every male has in fact a female pole, and every woman a masculine one, within themselves, as psychoanalysis again reminds us. This unconscious pole human beings carry in them as an openness, as a yearning, as a potential for recognizing the other sex and for being recognized by it and becoming aware of the distinctive image of God in themselves.

Normally, the individual man or woman will reach a position of equilibrium and rest in this bond with the other sex, which is the other half of God's image. The man needs tenderness and care, the woman strength and a secure anchorage. The satisfaction received in human love extends above and beyond man. It is something lived and felt as being 'after the image and likeness of God'. It points to Him whose most incomprehensible aspect it at least partly expresses in a clear sign.

In this way man and woman ascend to God Himself, by means of the opposite half of God's image in the other. This is where the possibility of sexual abstinence comes in. In the case of the adult not yet married it may be a provisional abstinence; for married people a temporary one; permanent abstinence in the celibate state, freely chosen for Jesus' sake. Every form of it makes available those interior energies that are mobilized in a normal sex-life. It enables a man to be a sign of God's Love in a different fashion, far beyond the possibilities of his own sex.

This becomes clear if for a moment we fasten our attention on Jesus. Jesus not only became a human being, a person, but also a man, a person of the male sex. That is not something either accidental or arbitrary. The possibility that God could become a human being was latent only in the male sex. The man, after all, is a symbol of God's mighty Love, the Love that redeems and saves. Whereas woman represents the humanity that God has chosen for redemption and bliss. That is why Jesus was bound to become a *man*. In the male sex the profound mystery of his being was prefigured: Jesus is the very image of the Father, His Love, faithful and strong, for human beings.

But there the symbolic value of Jesus' masculinity stops. Or rather, it is already as complete as it could be. To take one step further and enter upon marriage here on earth with a concrete woman, that for Jesus would have been a nonsense. In the mystery of His proper nature He, the God-man, has received more than marriage with just one woman could give. For it is He Himself who gives purpose and meaning to every marriage between human beings.

On the one hand the fulness of God's Love was in Him, God's tenderness as well as His toughness, for He was Himself God. On the other hand in His twofold nature, as God and man, He was the peerless marriage, the perfect conjunction, in His own person, between the redeeming God and redeemed humanity. In His divine nature He is the gift beyond measure, and in His humanity He is receptiveness par excellence. Thus in His emotional and sexual life as a man all tension was resolved. For His love was already satisfied and sated, was deeper and wider than He could have experienced in a marriage. His physical status as man-and-celibate is the token of this.

Therefore Jesus qua man had also to remain virginal. In that virginity of His, the conscious *and* unconscious sexual dynamic, the masculine *and* the feminine pole in Him, are put wholly at the service of the spiritual reality which He is and to which He comes to bear witness: He is the Son of His Father and His image; among human beings He is the firstborn from the dead, the new man, or rather: the Man, simply the Man, Ecce Homo!

Jesus' unique situation did not preclude a bond with woman. He counted women among His acquaintances, intimate friends, fellow-workers. In particular He had a mother; for like all human beings He was born of a woman. What is most remarkable is that this bond with His mother soon expanded into something much broader and universal. For from the very start every woman was more to Him than she was in her concrete and limited femininity. And all that she could be for Him Jesus had already been provided with in His own person. Thus Mary was not only His mother, but still more His sister, His bride, His daughter, and eventually His most intimate companion and the mother of all people.

We see in Jesus how sexual abstinence can bring out the profound spiritual reality of a person. It helps to lift man's whole sexual potential on to another plane, where it can develop and be fulfilled without ceasing to be male or female. This fulfilment of human sexuality far transcends the gratification of its transient and constricted eroticism—a fact that will surprise no one who realizes how closely the whole of sex is interwoven with the image of God in man.

Something analogous occurs, though on a narrower front, when somebody freely embraces celibacy for Jesus' sake, and in behalf of prayer. In his body and in his sexual dynamic something then occurs that both restructures his whole person and intensifies prayer and his bond with Jesus. If this were not to happen, celibacy would be a desperate hazard and in many cases could only make for a stunted affective life. This is why our celibacy would not be feasible apart from that of Jesus. Even then it is so only because He makes it our very special vocation. For our celibacy must be a sign that the new creation is beginning to dawn and that God has drawn close to man. Our celibacy is a call upon our complete sexual dynamic, as man or woman, and adopts it as a sign whereby our very life may demonstrate how everything is saturated by God's Love. Sexual abstinence for Jesus' sake presupposes a specific capacity for love—a widening, enlarging process so far out of the ordinary run of things that one is bound to call it charismatic. This happens in two directions. First outwards, towards greater universality. Virginity creates the possibility of entering into a love-relationship with all human beings. The unmarried person's family is the whole of mankind, the good as well as the bad, who are cherished and preserved by the Father. This first enlargement is an obvious one, calling for no further explication.

Sexual abstinence also enlarges the scope of our love inwardly, towards the deep interiority of our heart. Here we come back again to prayer and celibacy becomes a technique of prayer in the power of the Holy Spirit.

How is this? When somebody stops looking to the other sex to satisfy his need for love, then he has to find his inner equilibrium in a new way and settle with the opposite sexual pole which unconsciously he carries within him. If this process is properly directed, it can be very productive, even on the human level. It means that the unconscious anti-pole comes more into the foreground within the psyche and its affinity develops in a positive way. Thus a celibate man could in the long run be much more sensitive to certain aspects of life.

When the same thing happens from love of Christ and in the power of the Holy Spirit, the process penetrates much deeper into the human heart, to the point where the sexual anti-pole is the other half of God's image in it. This renouncing of the opposite pole encountered outwardly in marriage, if it is correctly done, releases in our interior being the spiritual value which that anti-pole symbolizes and which is unconsciously concealed within us.

Here we penetrate to the very heart and centre of our human mode of being. To where our psyche is still, unconsciously, sexually structured, after the image of God. But also to where God is already present with His Spirit, in His supra-sexual duality, beyond man and woman, tenderness and strength, *misericordia et veritas*. So celibacy throws us back on to the inner anti-pole of our sexual and affective life and finally on to God Himself with all the male and female components of His Love.

Thus celibacy can open up a path to prayer. In his plea for virginity (1 Cor. 7:35) Paul underlines his argument with an unusual expression which is difficult to translate without weakening it. He counsels celibacy because it makes it possible—literally translated —'to hang extravagantly around the Lord without being distracted.' This is perhaps the best description of what prayer should be. Many a commentator on this has emphasized how these unfamiliar phrases quite involuntarily conjure up the picture of Mary, who would sit constantly at the feet of Jesus to listen to His words, without letting herself be distracted by many household cares. This Mary from Luke's gospel (Luke 10:39) may well be the most suggestive 'type' of womankind and her unique femininity a very transparent symbol of prayer.

Of course, the prayer of the male and of the female will differ, therefore, up to a point. For sex does put its stamp on prayer. This cannot surprise us if we accept that prayer is assisted by the sexual solitariness of man and woman.

In his masculinity the man is more an image of the Father who gives Himself in His Son, and an image of the Son who proclaims the Word and loves mankind to the point of death. In his prayer the man will tend to identify himself with Christ and with the Word of which in his heart he comes to be the priest and celebrant. His prayer is a celebration through which he opens himself up to the hidden inner places of his heart, inhabited by the Spirit. There is his own warm modesty, the sign in his heart of that same Spirit. There he listens out for the Spirit, yielding himself to the depths of his innermost being, until he catches the Spirit's voice murmuring, stammering the prayer on his behalf: Abba, Father. So he becomes one with the deepest of depths within him and finds reconciliation with the other half of God's image in him. He integrates it into himself and in perpetual prayer makes it part of his experience.

By way of contrast the woman in her femininity is the image of the Spirit who is fecund, maternally welcoming, receptive, bearing and giving birth and cherishing. She is the purity that makes everything pure. She is herself inwardness and the love that descries the truth of people and things, uncovers and imparts it. In her prayer the woman, with all that capacity to receive, will surrender herself to the Word, be steeped in the Word, bearing an invisible fruit and transmitting life. Like Mary she will guard and keep the Word and will ponder it ceaselessly in her heart (Luke 2:19). The man apprehends prayer as a challenge, as a task, as a job, almost, to which he is committed and in which he finds his identity. The woman is herself prayer, in the very depths of her being is already prayer. In prayer she discovers her inmost personality, the ever springing source of her distinctive nature. So through celibacy and prayer man and woman find their other half in God. It is the other panel of the diptych, tenderness and rugged strength, which is a very rounded and entire image, here on earth, of God. Until God shall be all in all (1 Cor. 15:28), in the man as in the woman. And their body, spirit; without ever ceasing to be body, but a temple of the Spirit and a house of prayer.

This pre-eminently is the way of permanent celibacy. The married man or woman's calling does not differ essentially from it. Only the signs, the symbols, are different. In wedlock man and woman are a sign for each other of Jesus and of prayer, which still slumbers in their heart. For them, therefore, the path to prayer will normally be via their life-partner. What for the unmarried is engendered in the very act of renunciation, the married person receives primarily in the experience of physical sexuality. This is a very great mystery; it speaks first and foremost of Christ and His Church (Eph. 5:32). Thus they learn to pray together, to and fro, man, woman and children, because each is for each uniquely a token of God and its response. Prayer must always remain an especially onerous task for anyone who may not have been accepted by their life-partner in true love. Some experiences of prayer become from the human viewpoint almost impossible, even, for the one who has known neither the strength nor the tenderness of a real father and a real mother.

One's partner should not, however, be an obstacle to prayer. Because that is a possibility, Paul recommends for married couples a period of continence with the purpose of prayer in view (1 Cor. 7:5). For the other party, in flesh and blood, should point to our interiority and eventually to God, of whom he or she is the image that we too, carry within us.

So this is at once man's finest gift to woman and hers to him. That they awaken prayer in each other is the ripest fruit of human love.

Praying on a mountain alone

In the gospel we see how, when Jesus was going to pray, He would often separate from the others and take Himself off to some lonely place, a mountain or a desert (Luke 4:1; 6:12). For Him there was evidently a connection between solitude and praying.

We have already seen elsewhere in the book that solitude and silence are the normal milieu in which the Word of God has resounded to the full. Here we want to illustrate the link between solitude and prayer in a different way, that is, starting from the person who does the praying. How is it that solitude will awaken prayer in him? Only as he prays can he make solitude something viable and transform a desert into a luxuriant paradise.

Of course, all this will be true in the first place of anyone called to be a monk. But it applies as well to all Christians who in one way or another have experience of solitude, sometimes deliberately chosen, sometimes encountered involuntarily. Every Christian must be in solitude somewhere, with the duty of passing that solitude with Jesus. And anyone who tries to pray will often start by going off somewhere in search of a little solitude or silence. Solitude does not lie outside the world. It is a product of our world and inseparable from it. To enter into solitude you don't need to run away from the world, but only to steer clear of what is a well defined and outwardly very limited aspect of it. The solitary, uninhabited world is another facet of our world. It is one part of *man's world*. It answers to something that is in man.

Every individual has a certain need for solitude and a certain right to it as well. Most people can do with a bit of solitude and quiet from time to time, in order to express and live out something of themselves which may not otherwise come out and may never be brought to consciousness. When this need in somebody becomes an exclusive thing, we call him a crank. Yet there are certain categories of people, or of human situations in which a pronounced need for solitude is unsurprising and is even partly what one would expect. Among artists, for instance, or thinkers or even people in love. It is increasingly the case with the city man—once a year at least and sometimes every week-end—the man who just wants to get away from the world he usually lives in. So he chooses this, that or the other quiet spot where not many people come and, if may be, nature is particularly beautiful and affords a change of outlook. Can one say that he is escaping or getting *out of* the world? That is not what he has in mind. What he is after is something he calls a *green belt*; and this he unhesitatingly situates *within* the world, in that *world-of-man* which is meant to serve man and in which he will fulfil the best part of himself. The solitude of the green belt is to make its contribution towards the betterment of the individual. This can be experienced of course at all sorts of levels. Everyone will go searching for that bit of solitude in which he can best become conscious of, and experience, his need and his wealth of resources. The business man will be wanting something different from the poet, and both of them something quite different again from the man who looks for solitude because he would pray.

This urgent desire for solitude and silence has played a major role in the history of prayer up to this very day. In particular, monks have attained to a special relationship with the world by way of very concrete forms of solitude. They have fought shy of certain facets of the world and clearly opted for the pursuit of others, sometimes with a degree of pigheadedness. It is a remarkable thing that their flight from the world, so called, has always turned out to be closely *tied up with it*. They chained themselves firmly to particular places and landscapes: *Benedictus colles, Bernardus valles amabat* (Benedict was said to prefer hills, Bernard valleys). A twelfth-century Cistercian who had been especially zealous in searching out a barren and uncultivated spot took it as a compliment that it could be said of him as of one of his founders that he was *amator loci*, that he greatly loved his monastery and thus also the surrounding solitude.

Monks and recluses attached themselves physically as it were to the hut or piece of ground they occupied, so jealous were they for the bit of world where they were pleased to live out their adventure of the spirit. To say nothing of pilgrims and itinerant monks, who did not want to find a settled home anywhere here on earth but actually wandered the wide world, so witnessing to their quest for the heavenly Jerusalem. Their flight from the world was *within the world*; by which we mean that their attitude to the world is not in opposition to world affirmation and a genuine love for it. Such an attitude involves the world in the mystery of man and in so doing enables a positive valuation of the world to come into clearer prominence.

The world must give to each person space for living out his own peculiar experience of grace and for becoming fully himself. To the person also who prefers the world of solitude above that of human habitation. How does such solitude operate to the benefit of prayer?

The vocabulary with which the first monks describe solitude in the early Christian languages makes this somewhat clearer. The emphasis is often on retreat, withdrawal (*anachôrēsis, recessus*) and on tranquillity, internal and external: in Greek: *hesychia* (from which we get hesychasm): in Syriac: *shelyô* (inaction): in Latin: *quies* (rest, peace). All bustle and business stops (*negotium*). One has leisure (*otium*). One is unoccupied, detached and void of everything (*vacans*), in the most literal sense of the term: on vacation.

On vacation, however, for God (*vacare Deo*), in a solitude which one entertains in order to dwell in it with God, and so that the heart may awaken in the exercise of prayer. Each and every solitude throws us back upon ourselves and God, on our extreme poverty and God's immense love and merciful kindness. In this being made to rely exclusively on God's saving entry into the solitude, the faith in our heart is burrowed out and an unsuspected depth of our being is laid bare: that core of ourself where prayer is already given to us. It was in the wilderness, surely, that water flowed from the rock (Exod. 17:6), that rock which is Jesus Himself (1 Cor. 10:4).

How this process should be achieved in us will be clearer if we look again for a moment at how it was with Jesus. For Jesus too learnt something from solitude. His full stature as a man He first acquired and exercised in the desert.

Just as the people of God were tested and trained during their forty years in the wilderness, so too Jesus was sent off into the desert to be tempted and to learn there to live not by bread alone but by every word that proceeds from the mouth of God. By exposing Himself in the desert to temptation, Jesus involved the world of the

70

desert in His mission. There He inaugurated His Easter Work, His victory over sin and death. The evangelist Luke records how the devil left Him until the *kairos* (Luke 4:13); that is to say, until the time of salvation, until the Hour when in death and resurrection Jesus would reveal the full meaning and purpose of the world and of mankind.

In fasting, loneliness and temptation Jesus did indeed learn to be the complete man. There He thrust through to the very core of the world and of man. But the desert was still just a preliminary test, a foretaste of His Passover Feast, of death and resurrection. This is after all the etymological meaning of the word Passover: the *transitus Domini* (Exod. 12:12), the passing by of the Lord: the Lord who Himself traverses the deepest parts of our human mode of being, of suffering and of death and appropriates them, before rising from the dead to new life as the first-born of many brothers and first-fruit of the new world and the new creation.

Here too, in the earliest Christian thinking, lay the significance of His descent into hell. We must not think here of hell in the modern sense of the word, but of the Hebrew *sheol*, the underworld, or as Matthew so pithily expresses it: like Jonah, so 'will the Son of Man be in the heart of the earth for three days and three nights' (Matt. 12:40). It was there that the most intimate contact took place between Jesus, the God-man, and our world, whereby they are made one as it were, welded together in the Easter tomb. And out of there both together have become the beginning and the source of new, resurrected life.

The body of Jesus, sown in the earth, has impregnated the world with new life (John (12:24). Since then the whole creation has been groaning in the act of giving birth (Rom. 8:22). So far only the Easter tomb of Jesus has produced its fruit: the Lord Himself, risen in glory. But soon the whole world will explode into resurrection and new life.

Jesus' sojourn in the wilderness was an introduction to this and a foretaste of it. The world of solitude gave Jesus room to be tempted. As it turned out, it had a part also in His victory. Angels came down and ministered to the Lord (Mark 1:13). Only at this point did the world become completely itself. From being a world-of-temptation it became paradise on earth and indeed already a new heaven too—for where Jesus is present, the earthly and the heavenly paradise are one.

Thus the wilderness of Jesus already provides more than just a foretaste. It is already the Passover of Jesus in its first, not so far, elaborated form. The wilderness enshrines the very core of the Paschal mystery and remains for ever the symbol, the sacrament, of it. Whoever in faith enters into solitude for Jesus' sake is immersed in the Paschal energy that inspired Jesus' desert experience and later aroused Him from the tomb to resurrection. You will remember how monastic literature often compares the hermit's cell with the tomb cut in the rock, where Jesus awaited His resurrection.[6] Thus the hermit's cell becomes a sacramental representation of Jesus' death and resurrection.

In that sense we might even say that the wilderness is as it were, a microcosm, a sort of world in miniature where the world's final purpose is portrayed and made a matter of experience. First by Jesus in Person, and after Him by the people of God, the Church, in so far as in one way or another she feels the solitude, the loneliness, of her position as a diaspora in the world. This also applies in a special way, by virtue of a personal vocation in the Church, to monks and their life of solitude.

But also to everyone who for the sake of prayer goes in quest of solitude, if only for a short time. That is why solitude is so important. Early monastic writings stress this not without a touch of humour: you can throw over all other kinds of ascetic practice, provided you stick it out in your cell. 'One day, a brother living as a hermit in the Thebaid desert had this thought: What are you up to, being a hermit? There's no profit in that. Get up and go off to a monastery where the monks live together. There you'll be productive. So he got up and off he went to find Prior Paphnutius, to tell him what was in his mind. The old man said to him: "Go back to your cell, sit down and stay there, say your prayers every morning, every evening, every night. When you're hungry, eat; if you're thirsty, drink; if you feel drowsy, well, go to sleep. But stay in solitude, and drop this idea of yours." He then went to see Prior John and told him what advice he had been given by Prior Paphnutius. But Prior John replied: "You can drop the three prayers as well. Don't do any praying at all, but just stay squatting there in your cell."'[7] In another place it is put even more succinctly: 'Stay patiently in your cell and it will teach you everything.'[8] How can that be? St. Anthony sets us on the way to an answer: 'The hermit living in the wilderness, he thinks, is free from a threefold strife: the strife of the eyes, tongue and ears. One strife alone remains, the strife of the heart.'[9] This brings us straight back to our subject. For in solitude it is the heart of a man that inevitably comes to the top, with its innate discord: sold to sin (Rom. 7:14) and already indwelt by God and the prayer of the Holy Spirit. But it is sin which in solitary prayer comes first to the surface. Daunting, overwhelming.

This experience is in the literal sense of the expression 'dreadful'. Solitude shuts a man off from everything else and takes him back to his own nothingness. No outward show can help him any more. Every superficial prop, every distraction, has gone. A person stands naked and defenceless before God, that is to say, in that poverty and weakness which are his only asset. Before solitude brings him to the encounter with God, it first teaches him his limitation, his abysmal insignificance.

In literature and art the desert is considered to be first and foremost the place of temptation. And rightly so. The demonic spirits whom Hieronymus Bosch depicted surrounding St. Anthony are the externally projected images of what the hermit uncovers within himself: sin and frailty. In a sense the effect of solitude is a secularizing one: it gives release from many false ideas and illusions, from myth of every kind. It teaches one how to be an ordinary human being, frail and in need of help.

The first hermits were convinced that solitude enabled them to tackle evil and the devil directly. In this fight at close quarters, out of which prayer is born, God intervenes at the most critical moment, emitting His strength which then resides with the hermit. Through their lonely struggle 'the hermits send packing the world now superseded'[10] and something of the transfigured world becomes visible once more. Thus in the end the solitude reflects something of the deepest reality of the heart of the one in whom it unleashes that struggle; it is by turns wilderness and paradise, the tomb of sin and womb of the new world, the Passover of Jesus.

The way of solitude is strait and narrow, especially at first, as soon as the first flush of enthusiasm has passed and it seems clear just how much our heart is still inclined to sleep and how little our senses are as yet attuned to faith. Then it comes down to not abandoning one's cell and to persisting in prayer. This is something one learns, not from books but in solitude itself, and from solitude in those blessed moments when we have dismissed all else in order to be free for the Word of God and the urge to prayer within us, above and beyond every sentiment or emotion. Only the Holy Spirit can teach us how we may come to terms with solitude and silence, even to the extent that we can express the deepest part of our personality in it.

The solitary area that we occupy in the world should say something about ourself and our relationship to people and things. Solitude creates a new relation with the world. We experience and as it were inhabit the world in a new way. First and foremost that means our proceeding to live on a narrower basis so that a great many normal possibilities are closed off. And this we opt for. This deliberate reduction of some possibilities gives increased depth to other potentialities in us. It does not just happen, though. It requires a struggle, a conflict, and calls for a certain technique, ascesis. In the course of this process the solitude that we are coming to inhabit at an ever deeper and deeper level grows with us into a sign of the new creation.

Solitude is an easy thing only for the beginner who is still thoroughly sick and tired of the noise and pressure of the modern world which he has just recently left. But the desert is not only a place of relaxation, even if God is being sought there. In next to no time it begins to weigh like lead. It too can engender boredom; and one gets fed up with it. It fairly quickly presents itself as both inhospitable and uninhabitable. The moment comes for every recluse when he finds himself on the point of running away from solitude and giving up prayer. This is the hardest moment, on which everything depends, the classic temptation of *acedia,* boredom, dreariness (*cafard*, spleen). This temptation we can only withstand in the power of the Holy Spirit.

This is certainly not a question of willpower and human staying-power. Much more the opposite. They would soon put too heavy a strain on the solitary and even endanger his psychic equilibrium. It is in the first place a question of interior quiet, of freedom from all constraint, of equanimity, of a natural flexibility and of loving surrender to a peace that we carry hidden deep within us, but which can only break through into our consciousness in a fragmentary fashion. The slightest personal interpositioning, the smallest idle, ineffectual tension could be too much at this point and could prevent the very thing that was just about to happen.

We have to let go the reins somewhere inside us to a power which until then we had not been able clearly to recognize. A profound quietness, patience, waiting are then the order of the day. This non-intervening is of course the hardest thing of all. It purifies, even frustrates, the human drive within us to activity. This is where many draw blank, being stymied by the pride they take in their generous temperament and well meant activity. But only this quietness, this *hesychia*, can enable us to give ourselves completely to a far deeper and loftier enterprise within us. When the Lord appeared to Elijah in the wilderness He was not to be found in noise and great commotion but in the gentle murmuring of a cool breeze (1 Kings 19:12).

This is where the oppressive sense of frustration and estrangement that solitude arouses in us is so very helpful. We should not resist it, still less seek for distraction. Solitude evokes the sense of being uprooted and estranged. One feels like a stranger and a pilgrim, somehow apart from the inhabited world and en route to something else. One must not settle for a cheap solution to this. That portion of solitude which has fallen to him as his lot the solitary must exploit and fructify as a piece of the new world, as making a *home* with Jesus and the Father. 'Look, I am standing at the door, knocking' (Rev. 3:20); 'If anyone loves me he will keep my word, and my Father will love him, and we shall come to him and make our home with him' (John 14:23).

The Father and the Son, says St. John, come to make their *home* with us. In the original Greek text he uses for this the word *monē*, which remarkably enough is also used in the monastic literature to denote the cell of the recluse or the monastery where a number of monks live together. For this 'making a home with Jesus and the Father', this 'lingering' this 'remaining in Him' (John 15:4–5) are exactly what the cell will teach the monk who makes the effort to persevere and continue in it.

Anyone who thus embraces solitude has made himself unreservedly free for the dialogue with God. But to this God cannot immediately respond. Or rather, because He does not reach us satisfactorily at the level where we would naturally tend to look for Him, He must first try to divert our attention and draw it towards the deeper regions of our heart, the *'secretior recessus conscientiae'*, as William of St. Thierry has it,[11] where He Himself awaits us. Here solitude and silence will exert their most purifying influence on our experience of God. If we take care to ensure that this solitude is at all times a real solitude and that all other ways out are barred by thorns and thistles (Hosea 2:6), we shall intuitively, as it were, follow a path into the presence of the Lord who dwells there deep within us.

This will usually call for a period in which we are arid and disconsolate. Sometimes God allows our search for Him in the wilderness to be a lengthy one. He cannot impart Himself to us until we have repudiated every image and idea and attitude which fails to accord with what He really is, with the Word which He in fact addresses to us. This is why God is first experienced in solitude as an absent God; and the monk goes on all the time questing for God, as a hungry and a thirsty man whose dire need will never be wholly alleviated. The monk is by definition a never-to-be-satisfied seeker after God.

This searching for God, this yearning and grasping at the void the absent God leaves behind Him, brings the man of prayer very close to one of the most intense religious experiences of people today. He experiences God as absent. Words and feelings, after all, are too restricted to capture God, to incarcerate Him. The man of faith has no hold over Him at any point. Because he must as it were die again and again to his ideas about God and to his experiences that relate to Him, he cannot escape the impression that God is dead. This assertion is in line with the truth only in so far as it is the topsy-turvy expression of our own being inevitably crucified to the world and to every mundane notion of God before we can in truth approach Him. For no one can see God and live. He is indeed a consuming fire (Heb. 12:29).

The Christian's basic posture, therefore, is to 'stand and wait-in-faith'. He looks with longing for the Lord to come in person and reveal Himself. Medieval authors describe the contemplative as *suspensus expectatione*: lifted, suspended, inwardly torn with watching and waiting.[12] Here mysticism is at one with the conclusion voiced by a modern Dutch philosopher of religion, Corneel

Verhoeven. At the end of a dead accurate analysis of present-day religious experience he concludes: 'To wait is the only thing that we today can do with any assurance.'[13] The one who calls to God in prayer has absolutely no means to hand of persuading, let alone forcing, God to give an answer. But of himself he cannot even induce faith. He sinks further and further down into his solitude and state of abysmal destitution. The wilderness threatens to turn from solitude (*solitudo*) to desolation (*desolatio*). In the same way God's very own Son felt Himself forsaken by the Father, when He hung alone on the cross, in the sight of men and in the face of death.

Such human helplessness is a first product of solitude. It liberates a man from himself and from his all too human ideals. It reduces him to size in the presence of God. It lays a man constantly open to God's omnipotent mercy. Anyone who prays in solitude has in the end no other warranty. He stands utterly exposed to God's mercy. He is a suppliant hand stretched out to God, hesitant and trusting at the same time, a hand that God's love alone can fill. Meagrely, or to overflowing? Or after a lifetime of waiting? He must insist on nothing. He must utter no complaint. Yet in the night of which he no longer knows whether it is tending still to darkness or passing over already into day, he is more and more persuaded that God showers everyone, even him, with gifts far more than he dare ever ask or suspect. All this with the growing assurance that his Hour too is coming and that the Lord is very near. Slowly, before he is able clearly to perceive it, the desert bears its fruit in the solitary heart. Listlessness and a profound joy now alternate to the rhythm of grace. In the hour of testing: the purifying fire of God's absence or even of His seeming death. In the hour of His coming: unexpectedly, the shining of His countenance, like a blinding light in the utmost depth of his heart.

On the one hand, to be cut off from people, as the 'offal of the world' (1 Cor. 4:13), and on the other, the sudden knowing oneself again to be profoundly linked with every child of man 'in the heart of the earth' (Matt. 12:40).

Being dislocated and lifted as it were out of one's very joints, so as to lose one's life (Luke 17:33) and then to regain oneself and be permitted to recognize one's deepest identity in the new name which Jesus alone knows (Rev. 2:17) and which He utters ever more clearly in prayer for us.

Thus one learns, day after day, to dwell in solitude with the prayer that slowly grows within us; with its dismembering pain and its overwhelming joy. Solitude and prayer, then, fit together. There is an ultimate rapport between them. The one cries out for the other. They are akin. Solitude now becomes the familiar décor of prayer, the background against which the experience of aridity occurs and alternates with that of solace.

To be permitted to receive and able to conserve this gracious gift is the solitary's most onerous task. It demands of him a lot of humility, of quiet and of patient attention, a great yet hidden love. Solitude and silence have come to be much more for him, therefore, than mere technique or ascesis. They have become the tokens of his *dwelling in Jesus*, the sacrament of his Passover.

'The man who has not yet stood up to a long trial of solitude,' says St. Isaac the Syrian, one of the great masters of hesychasm, 'let him not so much as think of undertaking any ascesis on his own, even if he be a sage or a master, even if his manner of life be quite without reproach.'[14] For he will not as yet know the deep mystery and marvellous fruitfulness of being in solitude for God, and how each and every one can in that way attain to his profoundest 'I'. The twofold abyss of his own frailty and of God's unfathomable mercy will still for a great part be foreign to him. So then, our prayer inhabits our solitude; and the solitude carries our prayer as does the maternal womb its fruit—as William of St. Thierry expresses it.[15] The silence speaks of our barrenness and our abysmal destitution; and that same silence is sated with our joy and vibrates at last in harmony with the heavenly hymns of praise. For silence is 'the language of the angels', as the same Isaac has it. It is hard for one who prays, in the end, to live[16]—the element in which he is able to draw breath. In seeking it he is aspiring to withdraw ever further *ad interiora deserti*,[17] into a deeper solitude where he may penetrate to a still deeper level of his own interior being.

In and through him the wilderness yields its produce here and now; for 'God made the desert to bring forth flowers and fruits'.[18] The ripest fruit of the wilderness was Jesus Himself, when He went there alone to pray: after Him, every person who follows Jesus' path of prayer.

For him solitude is not so much a secluded region dividing him from a world that is passing away. It is his entry to the world-that-is-on-the-way and that will endure for ever. It is a passage, a thoroughfare, no longer. It is already *home*. The solitary is at home in his solitude as he is at home in Jesus and nestles in His love; and as he continues ceaselessly in prayer. In it he is at home with God, a repentant and converted sinner with whom Jesus elects to stay. So he continues sitting thankfully 'in his cell, with in his heart, unceasing, the prayer of the tax-gatherer'.[19] 'Lord Jesus, be merciful to me, a sinner' (Luke 18:13).

Watching and praying

When Jesus draws apart to pray, He prefers to do so by night: He stays awake, is vigilant, while the world sleeps (cf. Luke 6:12;

77

9:18; 22:45). Exhorting His disciples to do likewise, He speaks in one and the same breath of prayer. 'Stay awake and pray' (Matt. 26:41). In Jesus' experience these two things are inseparable. The example He set of spending the whole or part of the night in prayer left its mark on the life-style of His followers. The nocturnal vigil is something universal in Christianity, being a communal experience in the liturgy, a private one in personal ascesis. In ancient times ascetics and virgins in particular devoted themselves to keeping vigil, but Christians in the world did so as well. In the second century, for instance, Clement of Alexandria gives this advice to married church members: 'even at night we should frequently leave our bed and give thanks to God. Blessed are they who keep their watch for Him; they are like the angels, whom we describe as *watchers* ... We should not sleep right through the night; for after all the Word (Jesus) is a guest within us and remains awake.'[20] Later on, keeping vigil was held in reverence and great affection by monks and 'enclosed' religious. Thus Isaac the Syrian considers that the night vigil is quite the most important of ascetic practices. 'Should a monk for reasons of health be unable to fast, his spirit could attain to purity of heart and come to know the power of the Holy Spirit in its fulness just by keeping vigil. For only he who perseveres in watching through the night can comprehend the glory and the power with which the monk's life is invested.'[21]

Every Christian is invited to spend part of the night in prayer; but the amount of time is here of no importance. Even a very brief watch—going to sleep a little later or getting up a little earlier—is the work of the Holy Spirit in us and may yield fruit in prayer.

It is again the same problem that arises here. Again we are faced with a specific Christian technique of prayer, the constant tradition of which goes back to Jesus and the gospel. The same twofold question presents itself: how will keeping vigil, physically, help to promote prayer? How will prayer find a spontaneous expression in a concrete vigil?

We should not balk here at the ready and obvious answer; and yet that scarcely touches on the mystery of keeping vigil in the Christian sense. It is often said that night is a good time for prayer because it is usually quieter, that nature's mood of contemplation helps one to collect oneself, that darkness can conceal many things calculated to distract. Also that the human spirit, during the first hours after sleep, is still free of the many impressions which the break of day will bring. These considerations of course have their value. Just as celibacy gets rid of very many concerns; and solitude normally makes for interior peace and quiet. But naturally, arguments of this sort do not cross the threshold of the mystery. What is peculiar about Christian ascesis is just this: that its technique is completely geared by the power of the Holy Spirit to the dynamic of Holy Week and Easter. In imitation of Jesus, as He Himself underwent it, as a sacrament and anticipation of His death and resurrection. In our case this can only happen when the natural effect of the prayer-technique has been totally assimilated to the Holy Spirit's activity.

How then does the practice of keeping vigil help to bring this about? We said of solitude that it is a piece of world serving in a quite distinctive way to position the solitary in the area thus created. It is the same with a nocturnal vigil; for that is an out of the ordinary, peculiar means of experiencing the natural alternation of day with night. It situates the Christian, in a particular way, within the rhythm of time. Just as solitude has a specific effect on prayer, so too a special charisma of prayer is enshrined in this abnormal mode of experiencing the rhythm of day and night. After all, each day and night signify a step further in time, another twenty-four hours closer to the coming of Christ and His Kingdom. The Christian's whole life looks forward to that Coming. The same dynamic exists in the Church and is expressed in the liturgy. We do not know when He comes; only that He is already *coming*—not He who *will come*, but He who *is coming* (Rev. 22:20)—and that at every moment He can be standing at the door.

In the Book of Revelation Jesus is called: 'He who was, He who is, He who *is coming*' (Rev. 1:4). This definition of Jesus comprises three aspects of time: past, present and future. Note that 'future' in this definition is not: *He will be* as one might expect, but on the contrary: *He is coming. This* is the sole reality of Jesus that we are to be looking out for. Jesus is a coming, *adventus*, that which comes to us, in the etymological sense of the term *advent*.

If Jesus is always coming, then the Church is for ever 'on the watch'. She *is* a vigil. She is 'eagerly waiting' (Rom. 8:19–25) for her Lord and Bridegroom: 'So stay awake, because you do not know when the Master of the house is coming, evening, midnight, cockcrow, dawn; if he comes unexpectedly, he must not find you asleep. And what I say to you I say to all: Stay awake!' (Mark 13:35–37). So the command is always to be vigilant. No one knows the hour of Jesus' coming, only that He will come unexpectedly, like a thief in the night (Matt. 24:44; Rev. 3:3), and 'suddenly, as labour pains come on a pregnant woman' (1 Thess. 5:3).

We know too that His coming will coincide with a great ordeal, with *the* Temptation par excellence, of which the pangs of the woman in labour are an apt and arresting image: at one and the same time acute suffering and intense joy (John 16:21). That is why prayer is always conjoined with the alert determination not to give way in the hour of temptation: 'Be awake and pray that you be not put to the test.' Jesus addresses these words to His disciples at the very moment when He Himself, with the most crucial night of vigil that He has ever had to keep now behind Him, is about to encounter His Paschal mystery. It has been a cruel struggle, a bloody vigil and a battle to the death, in which He managed to utter the most decisive of prayers. He had surrendered to the free initiative of the Father's love for Him and for all mankind: 'Not my will, but Your will be done' (Matt. 26:42).

So the vigil, the watch that is spent in prayer, is grounded in the twofold reality comprising the end of the Age: the coming of Jesus and the 'great tribulation' which precedes that coming. That is why we are concerned here with a quite concrete nocturnal vigil; for the alternation of day with night is already, as each day passes, a natural sacrament of Jesus' coming. It is an earnest of what He is to bring. Night, then, is the symbol of sin and of the passing, transient world. Day is the symbol of the Lord Jesus and the age-to-come. Every Christian, therefore, is called in a special way to 'stay awake'. He belongs, in fact, to Jesus; that is to say, he is, according to the Bible, a child of the day and of the Light. Neither night nor darkness have any part in him. 'But it is not as if you live in the dark, my brothers, for that Day (of Jesus' coming) to overtake you like a thief. No, you are all sons of light and sons of the day: we do not belong to the night or to darkness, so we should not go on sleeping, as everyone else does, but stay wide awake and sober. Night is the time for sleepers to sleep and drunkards to be drunk, but we belong to the day and we should be sober; let us put on faith and love for a breastplate, and the hope of salvation for a helmet' (1 Thess. 5:4–8).

Day and night, waking and sleeping, this cosmic rhythm of the world and of man acquires in Jesus a new meaning. The night denotes Jesus' absence, early morning and day that He is coming. The Church, which lives in the expectation of Jesus' coming and in the assurance of His mysterious presence, does not sleep but keeps awake. Just as during His life here on earth Jesus often passed the night awake and in prayer before His Father, so the Christian will be prompted to remain awake and alert, so as to be with Jesus here and now. His keeping vigil anticipates the finished process of salvation.

More than that. As she keeps her vigil, the Church affects the temporal rhythm of the cosmos. 'In prayer, filled with expectation, hastening the coming of the Day of the Lord' (2 Peter 3:12). The man for whom the practice of keeping vigil becomes a way of life has actually found an original way of gearing himself into the alternating rhythm of day and night. In his night watch he is sustaining the expectancy of the Church, which is looking out for Jesus in the Holy Spirit. The power of the Spirit takes complete possession of his watch-by-night, which in a mysterious way comes to exert an influence on the cosmic rhythm of time. This is what St. Peter has in mind when he writes that in watching and praying the Christian 'hastens the Day of the Lord'.

To live in vigil is to begin to live somewhere on the boundary of darkness and light, where Jesus is always in process of coming. The power of such a vigil lies in the power of the prayer prompted and led by the Spirit within us: Maranatha, come, Lord Jesus (Rev. 22:20). It is the prayer of the bride in the Apocalypse, who awaits her bridegroom. Hers is a vigil of love, laying the world bare before God, piercing the heart of God and enticing Him to descend into the world. Then once upon a time, at midnight, the cry will go up: 'The bridegroom is here; go out and meet him!' Only those who are found awake at that hour will be able to go with Him into the wedding hall (Matt. 25:10).

That the man of prayer can affect the rhythm of time and expedite the coming of Jesus may perhaps seem far-fetched. We have another clue to this. The practice of keeping physically on the watch and wide awake bears its fruit in the heart that grows vigilant and begins to experience Jesus' coming with ever greater intensity. In our body's wakefulness our heart itself becomes alert. In the stillness of the night the heart too grows still. It beats only to wait upon Jesus. All other echoes and impressions dissolve. The heart is now all sobriety and attention. It is keeping its watch. Here again it is a question of that interior vigilance recommended by the Fathers, the *nēpsis* (wakefulness, sobriety) that uncovers the sources of prayer within us. Prayer is able now to make its entry. In our night there reaches us a certain reflected gleam of the approaching light, a first glimmer of the dawn. The Word of God is like a 'lamp for lighting a way through the dark until the dawn comes and the morning star "rises" in your hearts' (2 Peter 1:19). To watch with Jesus is always to keep watch around His Word. Here St. Peter gives the best account of a Christian vigil. The only light we have available in our darkness is the Word of God. In expectation of the Day's dawning Jesus is already spreading light deep in our heart, through the Word, like the morning star that heralds the approach of day. This passage is important to our subject; for it implies that Jesus' coming at the end of the Age is being anticipated in our heart here and now, as we keep our watch around the Word. The Jesus who, as we pray, shines in our hearts is a foretaste of the parousia, an inward Coming. In the night of the times in which we today still live the vigil spent in prayer is the first faint light glimmering in the world, a sign that Jesus is at hand.

Nay, more. For the one who keeps such a vigil Jesus has already come. According to St. Isaac the Syrian, 'the monk in keeping vigil is taking the shortest way into the arms of Jesus'.[22] Yet it is none-the-less a matter of being always on the watch and constantly on the look out for Jesus' final coming. Everything remains uncompleted and will so remain until the world's Hour shall come at the end of the Age. That is why our vigil is never over and prayer can grow and grow. More than any other ascetic discipline this keeping vigil is a token of that unfinished process whose perfection we can never achieve of ourselves nor yet exact from God. No one knows the Hour, not even the Son, only the Father (Matt. 24:36).

The watching and the waking jerk us out of ourselves and throw us into the hands of God, on whom all fulfilment depends and who will come at such time as He wishes, when a watching and a waiting world is ready for harvesting. So too with prayer. We can only be incorporated in the expectation of that new world, with body and with heart, watching and praying, till every temptation is overcome and Jesus Himself assures us: 'I shall be coming soon' (Rev. 22:20).

In watching and praying we live somewhere on the frontiers of time and eternity. 'He who keeps vigil mounts as far as to God's love and stands face to face with His glory.'[23] This is not simply a work of man. Is it not said of God Himself that 'He does not sleep and does not doze, the Guardian of Israel' (Ps. 121:4)? And in the semitic languages are not the angels known as *watchers, guardians*? Therefore, says the selfsame Isaac, 'the heart that wrestles in the night-watch' shall 'obtain a cherub's vision and have a constant sight of heaven'.[24]

And yet the one who keeps watch and prays remains firmly rooted with his body in this world. There is perhaps no other ascesis, even, that connects a person more intimately to the rhythm of the cosmos and thus enables him to penetrate to the invisible source governing it. For the material world too is invested by the Spirit and groaning for its redemption (Rom. 8:19 ff.). In keeping vigil a man shares this experience, this yearning of the whole creation. The Spirit groaning within the earth is groaning also in his heart. The watch he keeps lies open to the eager longing of the creation for its fulfilment, open also to the compulsive attraction it feels towards the Lord's coming. The prayerful watcher alone can give purpose and meaning to the world, through his prayer that articulates the universal vigil of the cosmos, through the vigil whereby he carries in his own body the birth-pangs of the new world that is being born.

'During the night-watch his eyelids bore the leaden sleep of the world. May there now shine upon his eyes the light that nevermore shall fade'—so runs a prayer in the Syrian liturgy used as a requiem at the burial of a monk.

Fasting and praying

Like the wise virgins of the gospel, we too await the bridegroom's coming, while we try to keep our lamps alight. The Word of God is our oil and bears us up as we wait. For the bridegroom is no longer present; and we have only the promise that He will return. The exact moment in time, however, is not known to us.

This fact of Jesus' absence and our constant waiting for Him find expression in our lives in yet another way: 'Then John's disciples came to Him and said, "Why is it that we and the Pharisees fast, but your disciples do not?" Jesus replied, "Surely the bridegroom's attendants would never think of mourning as long as the bridegroom is still with them? But the time will come for the bridegroom to be taken away from them, and then they will fast"' (Matt. 9:14–15).

So the Christian's fasting is a sign that Jesus is coming and that the great 'tribulation' which is to usher in the end of the Age is already at hand. Fasting played the same sort of role in Jesus' own life. In the solitude of the desert, on the threshold of His public life, the great testing undergone by Jesus went hand in hand with fasting—pre-eminently in the temptation which forced Him into a struggle at close quarters, as it were, with the devil himself, and from which, through the power of the Holy Spirit that had driven Him into the wilderness (Matt. 4:1), He emerged victorious (Luke 4:14).

Jesus fought this battle to the end, armed only with biblical sayings which He deployed as so many shafts to counter the tempter's insinuations, utterly alone in His solitude, all the time watching and fasting, in the inhospitable region which He always preferred in order to stand in prayer before His Father. Being alone, fasting and keeping watch around the Word, these were for Him the school in which He learnt to pray as a human being in this world.

Normally speaking, therefore, our fasting will also have to do with prayer; and both, with temptation and the fight with the devil. This is neatly put in a very ancient variant of the gospel text: 'some devils are expelled only by prayer and fasting' (Matt. 17:21). Although it may not be part of the basic text, still this variant expresses a very old consensus within the tradition. It may also rest on the personal example of Jesus.

Here again, this technique of fasting has to be completely subsumed within a spiritual dynamism if it is to succeed in bearing a fruit which only the Holy Spirit can give: namely, prayer. Of course, Christian fasting is not primarily a sort of dieting that functions to the benefit of someone's physical or psychological equilibrium. That is hardly adequate. The physical hunger must point directly to hunger of a different kind: for God. Bodily and spiritual hunger are harmoniously conjoined in a fasting which is undergone in the Spirit and only then can make any claim to being a technique of prayer. .The man who fasts will effectively discover for himself how it is that man lives not by bread alone but by every word that proceeds out of the mouth of God. Isaac the Syrian relates a remarkable but instructive anecdote. A certain monk had a habit of eating only twice a week. The other days he spent in a total fast; but he noticed that this became well-nigh impossible for him the moment he realized that in the course of the day he would have to interrupt his prayer and silence.[25] Fasting which was not geared from the very start to uninterrupted prayer became for that reason physically impossible.

The same author tells us that another monk had a parallel experience, but the other way round this time. As soon as he had successfully persisted in solitude and prayer over a certain period of time, he found that eating became a problem. He had to force himself to do it, and did not always manage it even then, 'for he was unceasing in free and easy conversation with God, without any strain'.[26] It is normal, therefore, for fasting to issue in prayer; and praying leads inevitably to a spontaneous abstention from eating and drinking. Here again heart and body encounter each other in a fruitful interaction. Together they ascend in a song of praise to the Lord.

How is this possible? Before fasting passes into prayer, and the one can no longer do without the other, it will have to burrow out new depths in a person's heart. Fasting affects him in one of his most vital rhythms: the dual rhythm of nourishment, occurring alternately as need and as satisfaction. From the very first moments of his existence outside the womb, man's being is structured by the sequence of these two factors. In this way he is able to stay alive and is gradually enabled to locate himself vis-à-vis everything around him. The newborn child feels hungry or is sated. Want and satisfaction, hunger and satiety, each with its characteristic aspect of pain and pleasure, are constantly alternating.

The more the adult person develops towards the ground of his existence, the deeper the need becomes and the less he is in fact satisfied by the material sustenance served up to him. The day comes when a hunger and thirst for the living God are born within him and, over and above all earthly sustenance, are engraved into his body. 'As a doe longs for running streams, so longs my soul for you, my God. My soul thirsts for God ...' (Ps. 42:1, 2; cf. 62:2). From then on only Jesus can fully quench his thirst: 'If any man is thirsty, let him come to me! Let the man come and drink ... He was speaking of the Spirit which those who believed in him were to receive' (John 7:37–39).

Fasting has a profound effect on and in a man. It can even hurt, though not to the point of injury, at any rate if the physical deprivation is truly indicative of a much more profound and spiritual one, which in actual fact will cost the person a great deal more: the absence of Jesus, the Bridegroom. Denying oneself earthly food means that even in our body we want to express our hunger for the age to come and for Jesus Himself, the Bread which came down from heaven for us (John 6:33). When fasting is experienced in that perspective, it sets going inside a person a process of spiritual maturation whereby he is slowly but surely switched over to the reality of his new existence, to his being-in-the-Holy Spirit. Let it be said, incidentally, that behind this again lie the significance and invisible power of eucharistic fasting. The tension is resolved only through sacramental communion with Jesus, just as, holy communion apart, the tension of fasting is relieved only in the intimacy of prayer with Jesus. Thus fasting and praying exert a very profound effect on a person's psychological growth. Up to a point they help to eliminate the traces of sin in him. For the psychological need itself, which is so blind and can often be so powerfully tainted with passion, is fundamentally altered by it. Indeed, the purpose in view here is not to fast so as to transfer the need for physical pabulum to the plane of spiritual pabulum. As a matter of fact, there can also be an indulgent spiritual appetite every bit as egocentric as the other sort and equally calculated to check the free activity of grace within us. On the contrary, fasting demands a great deal more. The whole point is to relinquish every egocentric appetite in order gradually to transform every need, no matter of what kind, into a patient and reverent longing for the Other, who can only give Himself freely and without constraint. Our more or less peremptory, demanding need for God, which really wants to shackle Him firmly to our own capricious inclinations, is transformed through prayer and fasting into a humble and expectant posture of being open towards Him. We can only call upon God *out of the depths,* without ever being able to take Him in hand (Ps. 130:2).

After all, God is not to be seized, as one might take and handle a piece of bread. We cannot imbibe the Spirit as we might drink a glass of water. To use a bit of psychological jargon: fasting and praying can effect in us a transition from *need* (le besoin) to *longing* (le désir). In the language of the Bible this means that we are no longer satisfied with the milk one gives to babies, but we are now able to cope with the solid food of the Spirit, which is the right of those who have attained to the measure of the stature of the mature man in Jesus (1 Peter 2:2; Eph. 4:13). So fasting and praying serve to express a great and purified love— the *castus amor,* the 'chaste love' of medieval man—which finds its expression in an unconditional surrender and in a patient waiting for the marvellous acts which, quite freely and without any coercion, God wishes to perform in our lives. As St. Romuald, using a very apt figure of speech, put it: the man of prayer is 'like a chick, wholly content with the grace that God dispenses (contentus de gratia Dei), who gets nothing to eat unless the mother-hen—this is grace (mater gratia!)—gives it him'. When every unconscious need has been refined into pure desire, God can respond to it in total mercy. A liberality which showers its gifts upon us free and for nothing, yet which we can never appropriate to ourselves: 'I look to no one else in heaven, I delight in nothing else on earth' (Ps. 73:25).

Fasting then is the source of unspeakable joy: the joy of the one who eats only from the hand of God. While our keeping vigil enables us to surmount time as it were, fasting takes us deep down into the unconscious layers of our being, where through the power of the Spirit we can hold our own against every want and every passion. In his watch by night man is like the angels who day and night behold the face of God. Fasting enables him to experience in his own being the deep hunger of the whole creation, a hunger that can never be appeased in a body, that the Spirit alone can satisfy. For it is the Spirit that time and time again gives aim and impetus to fasting and to prayer within us, and that responds to them both, without measure, far beyond every need of ours and every desire.

Praying as we live

This technique of prayer makes really deep inroads into a person's life. Prayer is not rattling off phrases and formulas or touching off this or that vague feeling. It creates *a new heart* in a man. Through his body he is geared in to prayer with every vital function and in all his dimensions: love and communion, eating and sleeping, time and eternity. Prayer is the energy of the Spirit, permeating and leavening a person and through that person reaching out also to the cosmos. In the innermost core of a man, in his heart, prayer is the echo and indirect effect of the 'striving of the Spirit' (Rom. 8:26) which is thrusting the whole world on towards the age to come. Not only the reflected action but the pulse-beat of the Holy Spirit Himself, where He is most clearly perceptible in the creation.

True prayer can never be accused of standing aside from life or getting lost in unreality. If any prayer deserves that sort of censure, it shows that it has ceased to be prayer. Pure formalism, perhaps, or sterile introspection. Real prayer is always located somewhere 'in the heart of the earth' (Matt. 12:40). It is the motor of all being, the hidden source of power that keeps everything on the go. The *soul of prayer* is in the most literal sense the *soul of the world*. The more it lives exclusively by the Spirit of God, the more intensely it will live by the world and for the world.

In the same context the question arises whether it might be better nowadays to talk about secularized praying. Did prayer not used to be too much of a sacral activity in which people tried to draw away from the demands of life and the world? An island refuge where a man could stand safe and sound with his God amid the hubbub of profane traffic. There are a good many forms of prayer nowadays which at first sight seem to be outmoded. People look for prayer that will bubble up spontaneously out of the ordinary course of things, will follow close on the heels of reality, cling tight to life's concrete events, to the little joys and setbacks of every day, to the battle for existence. People think that only in these things are they able to reach God. Other forms of prayer, through which in one way or another it is supposed to be possible to make direct contact with God, many assume to be suspect or seriously called in question.

One must readily admit that the secularizing trend has radically purified our notion of what praying is and has rid it of many false ideas. The God who only appears on the horizon to make things easier for man may of course well be an idol whose effect on man is to diminish him. And prayer that is nothing more than a bringing to consciousness, under the form of a projected dialogue, of our unsatisfied wants is fated to issue in the cul-de-sac of narcissism, self-contemplation and spiritual complacency. A healthy secularization will keep obliging us to repudiate our false 'I' in prayer and venture to face up to the living God Himself, He who is a consuming fire.

Secularization may, however, become a threat to prayer as well. There is a danger that it may make far too much of the human conditions of prayer. Then the emphasis is placed so exclusively on the technique as such that this gets in the way of all further development of prayer itself. Prayer does not get off the ground, never really gets launched and is given no chance of catching the wind of the Spirit in full sail.

This does not mean that a technique of prayer is in itself worthless. Far from it. This is equally true of the techniques of recollection and interior quiet now reaching us from the Far East. They can put us all on the road to prayer; but they cannot of themselves bring us to our destination. They have first to grow beyond themselves, as it were, exceed themselves in order to be taken up into the Paschal action of Jesus. This does not simply happen, all by itself. The technique must first be lowered to its zero-point. The man who applies himself to that will at some point see his effort break down, collapse, being inadequate to the task of prayer. That gulf between a natural technique and the *gift* of prayer is not to be bridged from man's side. Every technique runs up against the death of Jesus. It is faced with the foolishness of His cross. Through the faith of him who prays it can gradually be subsumed within the vitalizing dynamic of Easter. Then and only then the gulf is bridged by the grace of the Holy Spirit, which is able to turn every technique into a sacrament of Jesus' prayer and of His Paschal work. Whatever kind of technique it may be, it is no longer a merely human activity but a *miracle* of the Spirit, which He alone can bring about in those who are humble enough and know themselves sinner enough to expect everything from God alone.

Are we not wandering off the rails again at this point? This prayer-that-is-close-to-life, are we not letting it merge and evaporate into a sacral unreality? Absolutely not. On the contrary, we have moved much closer to the deepest reality of being, even though that central core does not lie on the world's exterior and is invisible to the naked eye.

After all, the contrast between sacral and secular forms of prayer is less than satisfactory here. Not that the distinction should be thought groundless. There certainly are prayers that have their source more immediately in the concrete circumstances of life, just as there are other forms of prayer that are meant to satisfy the rules of a particular genre. Yet this distinction is not so very material. Every prayer, whether uttered in a sacral context or not, must be adopted in us by the Holy Spirit. This is the only thing that matters: that we be guided and led in our prayer by the Spirit of Jesus (Rom. 8:14). The Spirit does not sacralize our prayer, any more than He desacralizes it .Whatever the prayer, the Spirit purifies it and makes it His prayer, in us. It is His alone to grant that our effort will rise above the absolute zero-point of the technique and will then flower in surrender, in a patient stance of openness to God's unpredictable and purely gratuitous gift. Yet the most inward of prayers is not unconnected with our outward life. We must now take a close look at that link for a moment. There is a degree of interaction between our prayer and our activity as people-in-the-world. In the first place it is through prayer that we arrive at a better apprehension of God's Will for us; while our surrender to that Will of God makes us even more free for prayer. In the second place, as we pray we achieve a more sensitive awareness of people and events; and this enhanced transparency of things in turn disposes us to pray the more. On this second aspect we shall elaborate in the next chapter, when we come to speak of prayer as offering and sacrifice. Here, though, just something about the link between the Will of God and prayer in us: that is, submission, obedience.

Earlier on in this book we saw how Jesus' prayer reached a culminating point in his total assimilation to the Will of the Father. On the other hand obedience was the stuff of His very being and of His praying, it was *obedience-in-prayer*. This also applies to the Christian whose prayer is directly focused on the concrete experiences of daily life. The person who wants to pray must make room in his heart for that 'perfect Will' of the Father (Eph. 1:9). That is why he has to discard everything that runs counter to that Will: his own constricted little desires, the shortsighted cravings that have never put behind them the narrow horizon of mere private interest. To learn to reside in the Will of the Father he has to divest himself of selfishness and egoism.

So obedience too is a kind of ascesis and may be regarded as an essential technique of prayer. For the monk this *labor obedientiae*, this toilsome work of obedience, as St. Benedict has it,[27] is even *the* ascesis par excellence. But one does not need to be a monk to practise obedience. One does not even have to be in some way subordinate. For obedience of this sort is not primarily submission to somebody else or to the *bonum commune*, the common good of a group—something which should also happen, no doubt. The main thing about obedience-in-prayer is the systematic surrender of our own will, the moment we realize that the Father's Will is beginning to revive with greater clarity within us. The things that cross us, the event not bargained for, others' predilections, in particular everything that hurts or vexes us in some way, these can be a sign to us that we are attached to something other than God and His Love. They show that for us an Hour has come again, an Hour in which like Jesus we can surrender ourselves totally. This dying to our desires will leave plentiful room in our heart for the Father's great desire: 'not My will, but Your Will be done'. For this personal will, in the sense of our narrow little cravings, is not really *us*. These things cannot express the depths of our personality. They constitute only our superficial, artificial 'I', which always bears the injurious mark inflicted by sin and reacts uneasily and awkwardly to it. Only the man who constantly rids himself of these whims and fancies and clings to nothing but Jesus finds inward peace. In him the Father's Will, hidden deep inside him, can come to the surface of his heart. The Will then becomes his own will. At last it is his food (cf. John 4:34), the motive force of his action, the one and only Work that he has to complete here on earth (cf. John 4:34).

The ascesis of obedience re-establishes a man in that 'simplicity in face of Christ' (2 Cor. 11:3) in which he was created. 'Simplicity' in the etymological sense of a 'single pleat': that is to say, there is but one pleat, one fold, within his heart: the Father's Will. He has become a new man, in the splendour of the first creation. Thus the obedient man is also a man of prayer. He has recovered a heart which is an irresistible spring of prayer. St. John Climacus has it, in the time of prayer the obedient monk is 'suddenly bathed in light and he overflows with joy, for thanks to his obedience he was standing on the threshold of prayer, and already ablaze'.[28]

The prayer which is constantly flowing in our heart also helps us to recognize the Father's Will in events and people. This is always a difficult task. In nearly all his letters St. Paul exhorts his Christian flock to prayer, so that the Lord may reveal to them His perfect Will (for instance, Rom. 12:2; Eph. 5:17). This presupposes a pure heart which has come to itself and has freed itself from every selfish and sinful excrescence. Then the heart is able to recognize the Father's Will, apart from and beyond all else around it. It sees, where others are blind. It distinguishes the depths of reality, whereas the majority lead each other on till together they fall into the ditch.

In prayer the illusions of our own will are unmasked. 'The sober and vigilant heart,' says Hesychius of Bathos, 'calls continually upon Christ out of the depths, with groaning that cannot be uttered. He who struggles so, sees the enemy crumble to dust before the holy and adorable Name of Jesus, like stubble before the wind.'[29] The purity of heart to which this surrender of the will leads is the same as that from which will arise unceasing prayer. According to the Fathers they both amount to the same thing. But if prayer can never proceed at the expense of obedience, strict obedience is sometimes preferable to the peace and quiet of prayer. So says St. John Climacus, whose view it is that God does not ask for totally collected, concentrated prayer from those whose self-surrender in obedience is complete.[30]

If prayer enables us the better to understand the Father's Will, it also helps us to penetrate deeper into reality. To a heart steeped in prayer everything becomes transparent. To it is disclosed the inmost core of being. In prayer everything points to God, speaks in some sort of His Name, praises Him unceasingly. Praying here becomes celebration. It properly belongs to a priesthood and celebrates a *sacrificium laudis*, a sacrifice of praise in which the creation discovers its profound purpose and meaning. We shall come back to this praying priesthood later on in this book.

Does this leave any room for difference between working and praying? Has my work, in effect, become prayer? To such an extent, even, that I may if necessary set praying aside and become totally absorbed in my work, so that in this way I shall be occupied with God all the time? A man's work may indeed become a constant occasion for prayer. Not that the prayer is in that case absorbed by the work; but because the heart of the person praying has become so pure that it can see through the veil that sin has thrown over the world. 'To all who are pure themselves, everything is pure' (Titus 1:15).

Of course this presupposes genuine prayer, through which one is taken down to the very bottom of the heart and is enabled to stay there permanently, watching and praying. A prayer that really never stops any more.

Is this feasible? By all means, yes—for anyone who knows from experience what it entails to pray with his heart, and not just with the lips or with the intellect. One and the same organ cannot be simultaneously occupied with two different objects. You cannot at the same time read a newspaper and a novel or listen to two different music records. But in the course of all this you can pray, amid work, amid study too; for prayer flows out from the heart alone. And only prayer can preoccupy your heart, down to the very bottom, the deepest part; and so it can become the true undertone of your being and of your actions. This takes it for granted, though, that that path is always going to be clear. Is it impossible, then, to attain to prayer unless it be within the heart? To ascend to God directly by way of things and people, for instance? Is not this another road to prayer, a prayer that is in no way aloof from concrete living but remains all the time completely rooted in it, a prayer that is born of life itself? In itself this is a possibility; and we would not wish to close that road off. Every created thing images God, and so can set us back on the road to God. All things were created in the Word (Col. 1:15–16), and can therefore speak to us of God; however much the image is obscured by sin, and the divine sound of things is spoilt by an obtrusive and excrescent noise.

However, the question is whether this road, without the help of the traditional technique of prayer described in this book, does not turn out to be a very long one, perhaps nothing more than a detour. For God does not only speak to us *in* things. He has given us His uttered Word in written form and His very own Word, the Son, in our human flesh. And both are ineffably near to us, much more so than any kind of created object: 'The Word is very near to you, it is on your lips and in your heart' (Rom. 10:8; cf. Deut. 30:14). And whoever believes in Jesus' Word, Jesus remains in him and he in Jesus (John 17:23). This is undoubtedly the shortest way: Jesus Himself. The treasure lies hidden in your own heart. You have only to pay the price, sell everything, if need be, with a joyful heart, and prayer is yours.

Seventh Chapter

THE OFFERING OF THE WORD

Liturgy inward and outward

Before we can go more deeply into how prayer is to be used in celebration, there arises the question of how liturgical prayer connects
with interior prayer. It is a question which we can no longer avoid.
It has cropped up from time to time already; and here and there we
were just on the point of stating it with greater clarity. For example,
in chapter five, when we were talking about the psalms. On the
one hand there is the preferred use of psalms in liturgy. They are
first and foremost a liturgical and therefore typically oral kind of
prayer, exterior prayer. On the other hand we are pleased to use
them in a private context. For many faithful people they are a
source of inspiration and the means of nurturing their silent, interior prayer.

This dual function of the psalm goes back to its origins. Of the
majority of psalms we can say fairly confidently that they were written primarily for liturgical use. And yet they have time and again
been matured and developed out of very personal experiences.

The psalm presents us therefore with the dual nature of every
Christian prayer. It is a public prayer; and not only the Church but
the whole world is implicated in it. Yet it is always an extremely
personal sort of prayer, it puts into words the ineffable bond between God and ourselves—something not to be shared with other
people; which is why we do well to seek the seclusion of our own
room and there pray to God in solitude and in secret (Matt. 6:6).
For the Word of God is simultaneously a public Word and a private
Word. It is a summons to the whole Church, and it addresses every
individual quite personally. What is celebrated in the community
must penetrate into the most secret corners of every heart and become a reality there. It is one and the same Word, the same 'glorious
course', the same fruit: the prayer that never ceases.

Until quite recently a clear line was drawn in western spirituality
between liturgical prayer and interior prayer. For some it was not
just a fairly sharp distinction. It had actually taken on the propor-
tions of a contrast; and sometimes there was even rivalry between
the two. Some rated liturgical prayer higher. Others pointed to the
necessity for interior prayer. But what did not emerge, for the most

part, was any precise account of how the two are interrelated. It must by now be clear from everything that has already been said in this book that there is no essential difference between liturgical and interior prayer. The structure of both is the same. In both, the Word of God holds the central place. The Word is proclaimed in the liturgical community; the same Word is listened for in the silence of solitary prayer. In both cases the course taken by the Word is precisely the same. The Word touches the heart, is received and assimilated there, and is finally uttered again through the spoken word or in the song of praise and thanksgiving—and this, whether it be in a communal or private celebration. In both varieties moments of silence play as important a part as listening to the Word. With the recent liturgical reform we have recovered those quiet moments in the official liturgy under the form of pauses for prayer. But in the celebrations of the primitive Church they were never missing.

The oldest monastic literature quite plainly refers to two kinds of celebration or liturgies which day and night succeed each other in the life of the monk. For instance, in his *Instituta* St. John Cassian has left us a detailed account of the office as celebrated by the monks of Egypt.[1] The communal night office consists in a Scripture-reading, psalms and silent prayer. After each psalm the whole assembly rises and as one man drops to the ground. Only for a few moments, though, for there is a real danger of falling asleep in that posture and at that nocturnal hour—as Cassian drily remarks. Then everyone jumps up and silent prayer is resumed in a standing position, in the time-honoured, classical posture for prayer. At this juncture the most absolute silence is insisted upon. Every futile noise must be avoided, even blowing the nose and clearing the throat! This is a sign to the president, and one of the elders, each in turn, speaks the prayer—the collect—which concludes one psalm and introduces the next.

However, all this does not complete the night vigil. When this recurrent sequence of Scripture-reading, psalm—every night twelve are recited—and interior prayer is finished, the monks hurry back before the dawn of day to their cells. There, says Cassian, they continue to offer up in private the same sacrifice of praise.[2]

Even now the liturgy is not at an end. Privately and without interruption they proceed to celebrate it in their hearts throughout the day.[3] That at any rate is the intention; and all the monk's fervour and effort are slanted in that direction. This is true even during periods of manual work, which will be picked carefully and must be of such a nature as not to interfere with this *interior activity*.

It must be abundantly clear from these passages that the structure of the exterior and the interior liturgy is exactly the same. The one is geared to the other. What each monk, along with his brethren, has learnt as it were in the communal liturgy he must celebrate throughout the day, according to his own rhythm, in the solitude of his cell. Here we have the vital link between the liturgy in church and the liturgy of the heart. An all too little known but very important document belonging to the Syriac literature of the start of the fourth century elaborates on that link between the two in a memorable way. The document in question is the *Book of Degrees* (K^etôbô d^emasq^etô). According to its anonymous author the one Church of Jesus is distributed over three different churches, each having its own liturgy: the visible liturgy in the church, the invisible one in the heart, the celestial liturgy before the throne of God. The faithful Christian must ascend by degrees from the one liturgy to the other.

First there is the visible liturgy which we celebrate in the churches. No Christian can do without that. Everyone must celebrate his offering like all other baptized persons and 'sometimes stand upright, then cast himself once more to the ground, either walk up and down or sing in the Holy Spirit' (27:5). Musical instruments are not ruled out here. They may be helpful to those who do not yet know how to 'praise with their inward senses' (7:16).

For the majority of the faithful, however, that is where it stops. And that is a pity. They have in fact been called to press on further and take their part in the other two liturgies: that of the heart and that of heaven: 'The Church here below, with her altar and her baptism, only brings to birth tiny children. They drink her milk until they have been weaned from the maternal breast. As soon as they have grown bigger, they make a temple of their body and an altar of their heart. So then they eat a food that is substantial and better than milk. This till they become perfect and able in all worthiness to enjoy the Lord Himself. These are they that reach the Church above, which will bring them to perfection. They shall enter in to the City of Jesus, our king, and they will be free to celebrate their liturgy in this most splendid palace, which is the Mother of all that live' (12:3). These then are the three stages whereby we may ascend from the visible liturgy to the heavenly, via the inward liturgy of the heart. Halfway between the earthly and the celestial liturgy, and sharing in both, there is indeed the 'church of the heart', where every believer, constantly yet invisibly, can celebrate his silent liturgy, the 'hidden work', the 'sacrifice of the heart' (3:14), the 'secret prayer of a heart that is fettered to the Lord and continues without ceasing to be occupied with Him' (12:1).

No one can pierce his way through to this silent liturgy of the heart without first having shared in celebrating the visible liturgy in the church. But if a man ever has succeeded in reaching the sanctuary of his heart, he knows from experience that he will catch a glimpse there already of the liturgy over which Jesus Himself presides in heaven. The heart looks out upon heaven. As Isaac the Syrian puts it: 'Make haste to enter into the bridal chamber of your heart. There you will find the bridal chamber of heaven. For these two are one and the same bridal chamber, and it is through one and the same door that you can see into both. The stairway ascending to the Kingdom is actually hidden in the depths of your heart.'[4]

Thus we should not call a halt with the celebration of the exterior liturgy and rest satisfied with that: 'the spiritual life does not remain restricted to participation in the liturgy' observed the second Vatican Council in a document that gave to the whole liturgy a new and very definite constitution.[5] The more vigilant our heart, the more ardently it will pray and the less inclined we shall be to stop short at the first degree of liturgy. For silent prayer is nothing other than the fruit of the liturgy. Of course, we shall want to celebrate the public liturgy better and better; but at the same time we shall feel drawn to spending more time in interior prayer. The two will gradually come to be related in reverse proportion. If at first we gave more time to the visible liturgy, we shall now feel a need to make ourselves totally available for the liturgy of the heart. We shall even spontaneously set about looking for a simpler liturgy, with less outward splendour, perhaps, but with greater depth and interiority. Such a need is normal and healthy; just as it is equally normal that the average parochial liturgy cannot and should not satisfy that need. Too austere and unadorned a liturgy would not succeed in attracting the ordinary Sunday churchgoer.

The tensions which this problem sometimes evokes have already been given an extreme embodiment in the history of the hermits and solitaries. In ancient times some of them actually kept themselves quite apart from church life and practically from any kind of sacramental life as well. As many bishops of the time saw it, this was not without its drawbacks. It was quite a time before the episcopate, in the third and fourth centuries, reached a measure of agreement in its attitude towards recluses who lived in the desert either alone or in small groups which usually did not contain a priest.

The problem existed too among monks themselves. Some were accommodated together as cenobites, in large communities. Naturally, the public liturgy assumed a dimension that threatened to absorb a great deal of the time that might really have remained free for private prayer. Other monks lived in small groups of three or four, or even entirely alone, as hermits. They seldom attended the liturgy in church, sometimes once a week, on Sunday, sometimes not even then. But for them too, the monastic tradition did not waver. Their offices certainly were authentic liturgy, but liturgy that could be much more simple, much more inward, and could confine itself to essentials: that is, to the simple Response which, precisely because it *is* simple, can be uttered in us only by the Spirit and which takes us completely in tow.

In one of his letters a certain John the Prophet—a Palestinian recluse of the sixth century—formulated the prayer programme for a solitary as follows. The liturgical Hours and the Church's hymns are excellently well suited, he thinks, to parish churches and large monasteries. But recluses should not have to recite an office divided up into bits and pieces throughout the day. They should apply themselves to constant prayer. This silent prayer alternates with manual labour, or rather should in the end be interwoven with everything they do. Now and again the work will stop for a while, and the recluse will stand upright, praying with arms outstretched. But even when he sits down to resume his weaving, his prayer will not cease. It will consist of a continuous muttered recitation of psalms, Scripture passages or short invocations: 'When you get to your feet, call upon the Lord and implore Him to deliver you from the old man; or recite the Our Father; or both together. Then sit down again to your work. You are to continue with your prayer until you come to the point of praying without ceasing, as the apostle requires, but for that there is no need to keep standing all the time. For your spirit should be in prayer the whole day through. When you sit down to work, recite psalms from memory or read them out. At the end of each psalm remain seated but pray: "God, be merciful to me, a miserable sinner!" If your thoughts get the upper hand, then say: "Lord, you see how hard pressed I am, help me."'[6]

To receive that gift of perpetual prayer is the monk's only desire, so that he must not rest content with the prayer entailed by the Hours. In his heart the interior liturgy should never cease. St. Epiphanius, bishop of Cyprus, received this message from his monks: 'Thanks to your prayers we have kept all the rules. Terce, sext and nones have been carefully and punctiliously observed.' But Epiphanius reproved them: 'So your praying stops! Have you no thought for the other hours of the day? A true monk carries prayer and the psalms constantly in his heart.'[7]

Through his interior prayer the most secluded recluse is in continuous contact with the Church here on earth as well as with the Church on high. His solitude is always busily occupied, says St. Peter Damian, who speaks of a *solitudo pluralis*.[8] However far removed he may be from the liturgical community, he is always *praesentissimus*, that is, the one more especially present, by reason of the unbreakable unity linking him with the Church, wherever he may be.[9]

A hundred years later the Cistercian, William of St. Thierry, goes one step further. In the famous *Golden Letter* which he wrote for the first Carthusians of Mont-Dieu, he applies to the relationship between interior and exterior liturgy the terms which Latin theology is to use for the sacraments: the exterior liturgy is *sacramentum*, the interior kind is *res*. The former is sign and token of the latter and finds in it alone its own deepest reality, its *res*: 'For the servant of God the cell is as it were a holy temple of God. For in temple as in cell one is dealing with divine mysteries, though in the cell far more frequently. In the temple the sacraments of our Christian faith are performed at fixed times, invisibly and as signs. In the cell, however, as in heaven itself (*in cellis vero sicut in coelis*) the very *reality* of all the sacraments is perpetually celebrated, in accordance with their whole truth and their peculiar structure, though not as yet with all the fulness of their splendour nor with that certitude which eternity alone can give' (1:11). Notice here the play on words between *coelum* and *cella*, heaven and cell. On the previous page of his *Golden Letter* William had exploited this word-play to underline the connection between the liturgy of solitude and the liturgy of heaven: 'What is laid up in heaven is laid up also in the cell. What takes place in heaven takes place also in the cell ...: being free for God (*vacare Deo*), enjoying God (*frui Deo*) ... Because heavenly mysteries alone are celebrated in the cell heaven and cell stand close to each other ... The way from the cell to heaven is far from difficult for the human spirit that prays ... The ascent from cell to heaven is often made' (I:10).

However solitary and secluded, therefore, the man who prays is never alone. His is already a celestial liturgy; and it continues to be always for the Church. It already penetrates to the heart of the world and to the core of all things. A fragment of an unpublished Syriac hymn of St. Ephraim (fifth century) describes this in its own peculiar and poetic vein:

He who celebrates alone in the heart of the wilderness,
He is a great assembly.
If two together celebrate among the rocks,
Thousands and tens of thousands are present there.
If three are gathered together,
A fourth is among them.
If there are six or seven together,
Twelve thousand thousand are assembled.
If they range themselves in rank,
They fill the firmament with prayer.
If they be crucified on the rock, are marked with
a cross of light,
the Church is constituted.
When they come together,
The Spirit hovers over their heads.
When they end their prayer,
the Lord rises to serve his servants.

For in the most solitary and silent prayer the Lord is present.

He 'sees in secret' (Matt. 6:6). He is Himself the High Priest of every interior liturgy. This same St. Ephraim cites an *agraphon* of Jesus—that is to say, a saying not preserved in the gospels but only in other very ancient texts which ascribe it to Jesus. In many cases these verbally transmitted sayings of Jesus possess a high degree of authenticity. Ephraim's *agraphon* is paralleled by another saying of Jesus which we know from the gospel record and which is often —and quite rightly—applied to the exterior liturgy. But this *agraphon* undoubtedly refers to the silent and interior liturgy: 'At the place where a man is utterly alone, there too am I.'[10]

The Sanctuary within: our heart

Of this silent liturgy the heart gradually comes to be the Holy of Holies. This is the climax of the process described in the earlier chapters. The heart, asleep to begin with, was first sought out and alerted by the Word. Fertilized by the Word, it came to full maturity. Incorporated now into the Word, the heart is consecrated as the temple in which the Word is celebrated in the most original sense of that expression: 'The heart set free from every notion, and moved by the Holy Spirit Himself, has become a true temple, even before the end of the Age. In it the liturgy is celebrated wholly according to the Spirit. The one who has not yet reached this state may, thanks to other virtues, be a good building stone for this temple. But he is not himself the temple of the Spirit, nor yet His high priest,' writes St. Gregory of Sinai, a Byzantine author who at the start of the fourteenth century restored contemplative monachism to full flower on Mount Athos.[11]

In describing this inward sanctuary the ancient texts commonly turn to the vocabulary of architecture. The heart is *an inner house* (*domus interior*), the *tent* (*tabernaculum*) *of the covenant*,[12] the *temple* of God in us, so that God is at home there and can never leave us again, because He cannot forsake Himself.[13] The heart is also a *secret living-room* (*secretum*), an *inner room* (*cubile*).[14] It contains a forecourt (*praetorium*),[15] hidden corners (*secretior recessus*)[16] and an innermost, secluded quarter (*penetralia*).[17] In the heart a complete cult is celebrated, albeit an invisible and wholly interior one, with a spiritual priesthood and an unbloody sacrifice. This priesthood of prayer is not to be confused with the priesthood instituted as a sacrament by Christ. It is a form of the baptismal priesthood which every Christian may exercise and through which he experiences the grace of his baptism. It is more especially in the texts deriving from the earliest monks of Mesopotamia and Syria that this notion is elaborated in full detail. The rubrics and regulations of this spiritual liturgy are taken from the ceremonial of cultic worship in the Old Testament. This in fact finds its fulfilment in the ceaseless prayer of the recluse. The hymn of St. Ephraim, already quoted earlier on, provides a very fine specimen of it:

They are ordained priest for their own sake,
the sacrifice they offer is their ascesis . . .
Fasting is their sacrifice, praying their night vigil,
penitence and faith their sanctuary.
Their meditations are their burnt offering,
Celibacy their peace offering.
Their chastity is the temple veil,
their humility, a sweet-smelling incense . . .
Their pure heart is the high priest;
Their meditation, the presiding priest.
Unceasingly their lips offer up the sacrifice:
the prayer that craves for rest.
In the mountains they sing of the glory,
the perfect sacrifice before the Majesty.
The song of praise that rises from the caves,
is the hidden sacrifice for God.
The depth of their heart is the Holy of Holies,
where is set up the altar of atonement.

Praying in the Spirit

This interior liturgy of the heart is entirely taken over by the
Holy Spirit within us. He conducts it. That is why its essential
features are evidently akin to the Spirit and to His activities in
us.

A chief and important characteristic is *liberty*. The more we let
go control of prayer and transfer it to the Spirit inside us, the more
sensitive we become to His interior leading. The sons of God 'are
led by the Spirit of God' (Rom. 8:14). This applies especially to
prayer. When we first applied ourselves to prayer, methods, rules,
a daily routine had an irreplaceable part to play. The person who
is not yet able to feel the Spirit—and most of us cannot—can only
be helped by rules and regulations that reflect what has been the
experience of some and pass that on to others. They have no other
value. They are not an end in themselves, but put us on the road to
the heart. They are pedagogues and tutors who help us to move
forward towards true freedom (cf. Gal. 3:24 ff.).

When your heart has really been alerted—and only then—you
will have no need for prescribed rules to tell you how, when or
for how long you should pray. Prayer has now itself become its own
norm. As you pray you will recognize the Holy Spirit who inspires
and incites to prayer. For a recluse, living alone, that interior freedom is a necessity. He should be able to surrender to the Spirit
the moment the Spirit summons him to prayer. In solitude the Holy
Spirit Himself moves into action, taking the place of the rules which
serve to organize the communal prayer-life in a monastery. Barsanuphius, a hermit of the sixth century in Palestine, wrote in this
vein: 'A hesychast (solitary who devotes himself to prayer) . . .

has no rule. Imitate the example of somebody who eats and drinks for just as long as he gets pleasure from it. If you are reading and you notice that your heart is impressed, carry on quietly reading for as long as you can. The same with the psalms. Where thanksgiving and litany are concerned, keep on with them as your strength enables you. And have no fear: God never regrets His mercies ... So do not go looking for rules, for I do not wish you to live under the law, but under grace.'[18]

The man who has been thus stirred to pray, and finds himself in the Spirit with a wakeful and vigilant heart, will normally speaking never stop praying again. As living water flows on and on for ever, so of its nature true prayer has a propensity for becoming *perpetual*.

This continuing prayer is a piece of the Christian's armour which Paul describes in the sixth chapter of the Letter to the Ephesians. It is the Sword of the Spirit or, again, the Word of God. We wield this sword 'by praying in the Spirit on every possible occasion. Never get tired of staying awake to pray' (Eph. 6:18). Paul elsewhere exhorts us to keep on praying (Rom. 12:12) or to pray constantly (1 Thess. 5:17).

This has then become the prayer of which you can no longer say that you are praying, because it has appropriated and taken possession of you completely, because deep inside you there is no longer any distinction between your heart and your prayer. Then it is the Spirit who is praying continuously within you and is sweeping you up more and more into His prayer. The more you are borne along by that current the clearer it becomes to you that this prayer is really no longer yours. It has become, so to say, autonomous. It is working in you flat out, under its own momentum. Nothing, no one, can stem this flood inside you; which is why nothing, no one, can impede this prayer. It used to be normal for you to find that the time for praying was limited; because after all you were far too busy, despite your sincere desire to spend more time in prayer. Now prayer has itself taken all your spare time in tow. It is like an irresistible force, seeping through here, there and everywhere into your daily routine. You never realized before that you had so much time to spare, that so many hours were being frittered away on useless things, hours that might have been completely free for prayer. All that time prayer itself has now released, immediately waylaid and commandeered in your life. Of this unending prayer you may even feel that it does not desert you when you are asleep. Whether you are thinking about it or not, consciously or not, prayer goes upon its way in your wakeful heart. The bride in the Song of Songs may indeed sleep, 'but her heart is awake' (Song of Songs 5:2). So too, he in whom the Spirit prays without ceasing. Not long ago a simple monk of Athos put it crudely but racily: 'In the daytime I pray with my mouth, but when I'm asleep, I go on praying with my nose!' He had surely been following the advice of St. John Climacus:

the Name of Jesus clung to his breath, and as he breathed prayer went along with it, up and down, in and out.[19]

Conversely, this prayer will never again prevent you from being totally occupied with people and things. For less than ever now do you yourself have prayer under control. Prayer has control of you, it carries you forward, undergirds what you do and what you say. In his *Vita* of St. Martin Sulpicius Severus uses a pictorial image for this. He compares the man who even in his work is invariably governed by prayer with a smith intent on striking with his hammer the red-hot iron on the anvil. The smith hammers on the iron; but now and again he deliberately strikes the anvil with the idea of sharpening the edge of his instrument a little. In the same way you press on with working; but every so often, without interrupting the rhythm of your work, you can slip in, unnoticed, an impromptu prayer. Work and prayer have grown into a single whole; and you have to peer intently to be able to distinguish the one from the other. As the same writer said of St. Martin: your whole life has now become *Opus Dei*, that is to say: a now unceasing liturgy.[20] In this prayer you are to some degree set free from created time and from its restricted rhythm. Another sort of duration imposes itself upon you from within. Something of yourself already exists *for always*. This is the beginning of the 'latter days'. St. Isaac the Syrian has interpreted this experience very accurately: 'The climax of all ascesis is the prayer that will never cease. Whoever has attained to that has taken possession of his spiritual home. When the Spirit has come to reside in someone, that person cannot stop praying; for the Spirit prays without ceasing in him. No matter if he is asleep or awake, prayer is going on in his heart all the time. He may be eating or drinking, he may be resting or working—the incense of prayer will ascend spontaneously from his heart. In his case prayer is no longer tied to any particular time, but he prays unremittingly. Even during his sleep it goes secretly on its way; for the silence of someone who has found his freedom is in itself already prayer. His thoughts will be prompted by God. The slightest stirring of his heart is like a voice which sings in silence and in secret to the Invisible.'[21]

Another characteristic of this interior praying in the Holy Spirit is its need for *simplicity*. After a time the prayer becomes frugal. The many words of the initial stage diminish into silence and die away. The man of prayer will restrict himself to a single formula, sometimes to a single word, or simply to the Name.

Where God Himself speaks in the Bible, He is always sparing with words, brief but incisive. The words addressed to Jesus by the Father are like that. Jesus too is brief with His reply. He Himself admonishes His disciples not to squander a lot of words in prayer. That only the heathen do, because they do not know the Father who is aware all the time of where our need lies (Matt. 6:7–8). Even the prayer of the Spirit within us is limited to a single cry, albeit one stammered without ceasing: Abba–Father (Rom. 8:15; Gal. 4:6). This continuous, rhythmical repetition of a short sentence is also exemplified by Jesus in the Garden of Gethsemane, where as He prays He repeats the same words over and over again (Matt. 26:44).

This *simple praying* found its way fairly quickly into the Tradition. The Fathers call it *monologia*, that is, a prayer consisting of a few words or even of one word only: 'Prior Macarius was asked: "how are we to pray?" He replied: "Unnecessary to devote a lot of words to it. It's enough to spread your hands and say: "Lord, as you please and as you know, have pity." If the struggle grows fiercer, then say: 'Lord, help me!' After all, He knows what you have need of, and will take pity on you." '[22]

This tradition has been a constant one in the East as in the West. Out of it was to come, with the passage of time, the kind of ejaculatory prayer with which Cassian seems to have already been familiar, short little prayers that require little time and effort but are much to the point.[23] Cassian liked best the verse from the psalm: 'God, come to my aid, Lord, hasten to help me' Ps. 70:2), the advantages of which he describes from every angle. Others prefer briefer exclamations, which they often borrow from the gospel. Thus for instance St. John Climacus: 'let your prayer be simple and without many words: one word was enough to procure forgiveness for the tax-gatherer and the prodigal son ... Don't go chasing after this or that form of words in your prayer. A child's simple and monotonous stuttering is enough to carry conviction with father. Don't be long-winded. You will distract your mind if you go searching for words. One word from the tax-gatherer moved God to compassion. A single word of faith saved the good murderer. Lengthy prayers build up all sorts of images in the mind and distract it, whereas a single word (*monologia*) can bring it to a state of recollection. If you feel that by uttering a word you are inwardly comforted and mollified, stay with that word, for then your angel is praying with you.'[24]

What we have here once more is the technique of the *lectio*, as described in chapter four. You can apply it to these invocations as well. A lot of brief, ejaculatory prayers preserved in the Bible can be used to back up your prayer. The gospels and the psalms are a goldmine. For each time of prayer you can find your own form of words or ejaculatory prayer, or you can create it, as you listen to your heart and to the Holy Spirit, who stirs you within: 'Lord Jesus, I believe, help my unbelief—Lord Jesus, that I may see—Lord Jesus, you know that I love you—Lord Jesus, not my will but your will, and so forth.' The list is endless, and each saying, each word, is inexhaustible, in the light and in the power of the Holy Spirit. So long as one of these formulas keeps your heart on the go, you must not drop it. Quietly persist with it, until your heart is totally on fire within, the moment God so pleases.'

Try too, perhaps, to breathe at the rhythm of your exclamation. In that way your body's resonance will answer to the pulse-beat of your prayer; and so you will breathe back to God the Word of God that the Spirit has breathed out to you in Scripture. A Flemish mystical author of the seventeenth century, Maria Petyt, calls this the 'inspiriting process'. Through the Word of your prayer your own living spirit is mingled with the Spirit of God. What the Byzantine tradition knows as the Jesus-prayer is one instance of those many possibilities. It is also a prayer that has become *monologistos*, single-worded, simple, around the Name of Jesus and an especially telling sentence from the gospel, in this case the tax-gatherer's prayer: 'Have mercy on me, a wretched sinner!' It is most certainly one of the best formulas; for it is our response to the essential message of the gospel: that we are sinners and that Jesus comes to bring us forgiveness.

In the Jesus-prayer, besides the cry of the tax-gatherer the Name of Jesus itself has an important part to play. Actually, it can be even simpler still, in that the Jesus-prayer may well be reduced to the simple invocation of Jesus' Name. For the Name of Jesus is charged with an invisible and unsuspected power: strength in temptation, and consolation where there is a yearning for love. 'The manifold repetition of this Name, the blessed Aelred writes to his hermitess sister, 'pierces our heart from within.'[25]

The Name of Jesus, or the *dulcis memoria* of Jesus, the sweet remembrance of His Name, stands in fact for the very presence of Jesus. For together with His Name Jesus comes into our heart in person and lodges there. In particular it is Hesychius of Bathos—a medieval Byzantine author rather difficult to place—who has described this technique with great affection: 'The ceaseless invocation of Jesus, put alongside an ardent and joyous longing for Him, fills our heart's atmosphere with joy and peace. All this thanks to a strict, interior concentration ... The recollection of Jesus and the unremitting invocation of His Name create as it were a divine atmosphere in our spirit, provided we do not stop calling inwardly upon Jesus and that we continue in sobriety and watchfulness. Let us remain true at all times and in all places to this task of calling upon the Lord Jesus. Let us cry out to Him with heart aflame so that we may appropriate the holy Name of Jesus ... We should not cease to toss about the Name of Jesus in the spaces of our heart, as the lightning darts to and fro in the firmament as soon as rain is on the way ... Blessed the spirit that is wholly given to the Jesus-prayer. Blessed the heart in which the Name of Jesus ceaselessly resounds, as inseparably as the air cleaves to our body and the flame to the candle. The sun, moving across the firmament, engenders the day; the holy Name of Jesus, constantly appearing in our spirit, brings forth glorious notions without number.'[26]

This calling upon the Name of Jesus is actually a *calling-in* of Jesus Himself. The Blessed Ruisbroek uses this term to describe an analogous technique of prayer. He also calls it the *summoning-in*, the *importuning*, of Jesus. In this guise the Jesus-prayer has been disseminated not only in the Christian East. It turns up just as frequently in the West, though less systematically than was the case in the East during the thirteenth and fourteenth centuries. One has only to think here of St. Bernard, for whom the Name of Jesus, in line with the passage in the Song of Songs (1:3), is an oil outpoured. Like oil, the Name gives light and warmth, it is nourishment and medicine.[27] Synthesized and in a poetic form, the most important of these themes have since been brought together in the well known medieval hymn: *Jesu dulcis memoria*.

Invoking the Name of Jesus, therefore, very much resembles a spiritual communion. It strengthens and feeds you. It imparts to you Jesus Himself, who obtains an ever firmer footing in your heart. In the end the Name does more than express your own ardent longing for Jesus. It is the very Love of Jesus in you, an uncreated light, a consuming fire. This was the prayer that William of St. Thierry recommended to the first Carthusians: 'During the prayer you must go and stand before God, face to face, and examine yourself in the light of His countenance. Then you will call on the Name of the Lord and with that Name strike upon the stone of your heart till fire leaps from it. You will keep fluttering about the recollection of the abundance of God's sweetness till He Himself causes that sweetness to well up within your heart.'[28]

Cosmic prayer

As for this interior liturgy it must have become abundantly clear by now that it is not a private affair between God and yourself. The whole world is involved in it. Prayer is a cosmic enterprise for which certain people may make themselves totally free, so as to be able to devote themselves to it.

That you have become a free human being, that your heart has begun to live and to sing, that the Word of God is able to reverberate freely and frankly in your inmost centre, is a source of light and power for anyone. What has happened to you is a fragment of salvation history, and has also happened to the Church and to the world. God has found a space here on earth where He can be Himself, where He can play and enjoy Himself with a child of man. Humanity has once more discovered a source from which God can cause water to well up for all who thirst. For the deepest depth of your heart is also the deep ground of the world.

In this experience of prayer the world's spatial limits are eliminated. Being far off or being close at hand no longer signifies. Being absent and being present have become one and the same thing. In your prayer all human beings are closely involved. As one of the Fathers put it so emphatically: 'The monk is the man separated from everyone and bound up with everyone.'[29] For by way of prayer you already inhabit the deep heart of the cosmos.

Yet another example of this is the fact that a modern thinker like Teilhard de Chardin, who is justifiably considered to be the pioneer of Christian affirmation of the world, saw in contemplative prayer the most intense and productive form of world solidarity: 'In one of his stories Robert Hugh Benson tells of a "visionary" coming on a lonely chapel where a nun is praying. He enters. All at once he sees the whole world bound up and moving and organizing itself around that out-of-the-way spot, in tune with the intensity and inflection of the desires of that puny, praying figure. The convent chapel had become the axis about which the earth revolved. The contemplative sensitized and animated all things because she believed; and her faith was operative because her very pure soul placed her near to God.' Teilhard subsequently comments on that parable: 'If we want the divine *milieu* to grow all around us, then we must jealously guard and nourish all the forces of union, of desire and of prayer that grace offers us. By the mere fact that our transparency will increase, the divine light, that never ceases to press in upon us, will irrupt the more powerfully.'[30] In another passage Teilhard describes the man of prayer in these terms: 'Seeing the mystic immobile, crucified or rapt in prayer, some may perhaps think that his activity is in abeyance or has left this earth: they are mistaken. Nothing in the world is more intensely alive and active than purity and prayer, which hang like an unmoving light between the universe and God.

Through their serene transparency flow the waves of creative power charged with natural virtue and with grace. What else but this is the Virgin Mary.'[31]

Even in his time St. John Chrysostom recognized in these *prayerful* souls 'the Fathers of the whole of mankind, who give thanks for the whole world.'[32] 'They pray for the world, and in that way provide the most telling proof of their friendship;' for 'of His exceeding great goodness God often confers salvation on a large mass, for the sake of just a few righteous people.'[33] There are instances of this even nowadays, as we know. A recluse who was asked not long ago how even in total solitude he was able to feel inextricably linked with the world and with other people, replied without any hesitation: 'Every time I extend my arms in prayer to God, I feel that at the same time I am holding the entire world in my embrace.' And indeed he was living at the time on a mountain in Chile, where the Andes were all that he could see.

But this *cosmic prayer* is not restricted to the business of praying for the world. Such intercession is doubtless very potent. But prayer does still more. It cleanses people and things. It lays their deep centre bare; and in so doing prayer restores and heals the creation, sees it in the light of God and brings it back to Him. That is why every prayer is always related with *blessing*; and it will normally overflow into eucharistia, *thanksgiving*.

Because by praying he has found deep within his heart his true self, the man of prayer may now perhaps be able to identify everything else. He has acquired a new way of looking at people and things. From within his own centre he reaches also to the centre of all that comes in his direction. And again, he is more sensitive to the mask that others put upon us, to everything that hinders the world from being itself before God. The Greek authors call such a person *diaratikos*, meaning that he *sees through* the outward appearance of people and things. The veil of egoism is for him already lifted. He *perceives* it all. As Isaac the Syrian wrote: 'he surveys the flame of things'.

He alone, therefore, is really in a position to thank God for the creation and to offer Him a sacrifice of praise on behalf of mankind. This is a main task of every baptized person. Paul is for ever urging them to undertake it. The Christian should 'spill over with thanksgiving' (Col. 2:7). Whatever the circumstances, he is to give thanks, for this is the Will of God (1 Thess. 5:18). He is to 'go on singing and chanting to the Lord' in his heart, so that always and everywhere he is 'giving thanks to God who is our Father in the name of our Lord Jesus Christ' (Eph. 5:18–20). Even petitionary prayer and intercession on behalf of others are to be uttered before God 'along with thanksgiving' (Phil. 4:6).

This is a new and very important aspect of cosmic prayer in the Holy Spirit. It hallows things and makes them an expression of thanks, a kind of grace. 'Everything God has created is good, and no food is to be rejected, provided grace is said for it: the Word of God and the prayer make it holy' (1 Tim. 4:4–5)). Everything that can be incorporated in such thanksgiving thereby attains its ultimate purpose and as a sacrifice of praise is thus returned into the presence of the Father. In this way everything comes to be truly understood as the pure gift of the Father of all light, descending into our hands. Our hands do not close around that gift. Quite the contrary. In our hands it becomes the sacrifice of mankind, offered to the Father. In our heart and on our lips it flows back to the Father, as an act of thanksgiving.[34]

It is the crown and climax of prayer. Isaac the Syrian has put an otherwise unknown definition of prayer into the mouth of Jesus: it is a 'joy that mounts up to God in thanksgiving'.

Just as the first Adam, prior to the Fall, was able to give all creatures a name that would precisely express their identity, so in his turn the Christian can utter in prayer something of the *new name* that will be given to all things by Jesus, the second Adam

(Rev. 3:12). For that new name lies enclosed within the Name of Jesus which you can lay as a benediction on everything that passes through your hands, on every person you meet, on every face that is turned in your direction. Contact, with a prayer. Meeting, with a benediction. So you will become able to recognize the new identity of man and world, along with Jesus. At some time or other in his life each of us has met a man of God from whom he has received the selfsame thing, whose look has pierced him like a tongue of flame, charged with the tenderness of God and with His purifying strength.

Anyone able to utter over the world a prayer of thanksgiving can also make use of that world without being seduced or overwhelmed by it. St. Paul calls this 'using the world without abusing it' (1 Cor. 7:31). For in prayer you can gauge precisely the value of the creation, God's gift and God's reflection, man's sacrificial offering. It all flowers open into a ceaseless thanksgiving. The story is told of the Church Father, Arsenius, that each year, at harvest time, he caused his disciples to bring him fruit, one sample of each kind: 'He would accept it and would eat it up, giving thanks the while.'[35]

At this point the Christian's prayer grows into a celebration in which the whole creation shares. It becomes a festive *observance* of everything that can be approached or experienced. So we come back once more to what we instanced earlier on as a sort of priesthood of prayer. If prayer is the interior worship and liturgy of the heart, with an invisible altar and a hidden sacrifice, then each praying individual conducts the liturgy of his own prayer and is the priest of this burnt-offering-within. For just as Jesus, before the face of His Father 'is living for ever to intercede for us' (Heb. 7:25) and as a priest for ever there celebrates his sacrifice, so must every Christian offer the like sacrifice of prayer: 'Through Him, let us offer God an unending sacrifice of praise, a verbal sacrifice that is offered every time we acknowledge His Name' (Heb. 13:15). This priesthood and this sacrifice are for the whole world.

There could be no better way of rounding off this chapter than by attending once more to the hymn by St. Ephraim with which we are already familiar. He is again talking about the hermits' prayer:

They have been ordained priests of the hidden mysteries,
  and make up for our frailties.
Unseen they pray for our faults,
  and stand erect, entreating for our acts of foolishness . . .
The mountains have become torches,
All and sundry are flocking toward them.
Where one of them is to be found,
  those around him end up reconciled.
They are strongholds in the desert,
  thanks to them we are in peace.

THE LUTE-PLAYER

Is praying difficult?

A fourteenth-century Byzantine monk, who for a short time was Patriarch of Constantinople with the name of Callixtus II, answers this question with the illustration of the lute-player.[1] 'The lute-player bends over his instrument and listens attentively to the tune, while his fingers manipulate the plectrum and make the strings vibrate in full-toned harmony. The lute has turned into music; and the man who strums upon it is taken out of himself, for the music is soft and entrancing.'

Anyone who prays must set about it in the same way. He has a lute and a plectrum at his disposal. The lute is his heart, the strings of which are the inward senses. To get the strings vibrating and the lute playing he needs a plectrum, in this case: the recollection of God, the Name of Jesus, the Word. So the lute-player has to listen attentively and vigilantly to his heart and pluck its strings with the Name of Jesus. Until the senses open up and his heart becomes alert. The person who strums incessantly upon his heart with the Name of Jesus sets his heart a' singing, 'an ineffable happiness flows into his soul, the recollection of Jesus purifies his spirit and makes it sparkle with divine light'.

Is praying difficult?

No one is going to give you the answer to that question. This short book has no answer for you, either. It cannot pretend to be an introduction to prayer, much less a manual of instruction. We have been listening together to the witness of a centuries'-old tradition of prayer in the Church of Jesus. Something may have revealed itself to you on the way. Has the Spirit of Jesus, who never ceases from praying in your heart, suddenly disclosed and avowed Himself? Like the embryo that leapt in the womb of Elizabeth when it encountered Jesus in Mary's womb?

If not, that is no reason to feel discouraged: your Hour is still to come.

If so, then you should give everything you have to the task of catching more clearly the still sound of God within you. For there the field lies, and there the treasure is hidden. The moment you discover the treasure of prayer in the field of your heart, you will go off full of joy and sell all that you possess in order to have that treasure. And the lute is at your disposal, and the plectrum too. These are your heart, and the Word of God. The Word is, after all, very close to you, on your lips and in your heart (Rom. 10:8).

You need only pick up the plectrum and pluck the strings. To persevere in the Word and in your heart, watching and praying. There is no other way of learning how to pray. You must return to yourself and to your true and deepest nature, to the human-being-in-Jesus that you already are, purely and simply by grace. 'Nobody can learn how to see. For seeing is something we can do by nature. So too with prayer. *Authentic prayer* can never be learnt from someone else. It has its own instructor within it. Prayer is God's gift to him who prays.'[2]

Katsberg, 1971.

NOTES

First chapter
1. Apophthegms, Anthony, 7.
2. Anthony, cited by Cassian, Coll., 9, 31.

Second chapter
1. Apophthegms, Latin collection, 21, 14.
2. Guigo I the Carthusian, Vita S. Hugonis, 12.
3. Dial. II, 3.
4. Guigo I the Carthusian, Meditationes, 4.
5. Hesychius of Bathos, Centurie, II, 3.

Third chapter
1. Apophthegms, Arsenius, 27.

Fourth chapter
1. An unknown monk of the 13th century, Meditatio de Passione et Resurrectione Christi, 38; P.L. 184, 766.
2. Giogo II the Carthusian, second meditation.
3. Pap. III. A, 73.
4. Meditation 12.
5. Evagrius, Hypotyposis.
6. Letter, 29.
7. Guerricus, Sermon 5, for Christmas.
8. Rudolph of Camaldoli, Constitutiones.
9. Logos, 66.
10. Apophthegms, Latin collection, 21, 14.
11. Apophthegms, Agathon, 9.
12. Evagrius, Rerum mon. rat., 11.
13. Cf. Hesychius of Bathos, Centurie, 97.
14. Hesychius of Bathos, Centurie, I, 93.
15. Macariana, cited by J. Gouillard, Petite Philocalie, pp. 53–4

Sixth chapter
1. Apophthegms, Agathon, 8.
2. Anthony, Letter 1.
3. Apophthegms, Longinus, no. 5.
4. Evagrius, Spec. mon., 39–43.
5. Rule of St. Benedict, c. 49.
6. E.g., Peter Damian, Dominus vobiscum, 19: 'O little cell, almost a

competitor of the Lord's sepulchre, you who welcome those who are dead in sin, and revive them with the breath of the Holy Spirit!'

7. Apophthegms, Paphnutius, 5.
8. Apophthegms, Moses, 6.
9. Apophthegms, Anthony, 11.
10. Ammonas, letter 12 (Syriac series).
11. Golden Letter, II, 1.
12. Guerricus, Sermo 1 de Adventu.
13. *Rondom de leegte*, end.
14. Logos 13.
15. Golden Letter, I, 11.
16. Apophthegms, Anthony, 10.
17. Vita Antonii, 29.
18. Eucherius of Lyons, De laude eremi, 5.
19. Apophthegms, Ammonas, 4.
20. Paedag. II, 79, 2 and 81, 4.
21. Logos 29.
22. Logos 29.
23. Isaac the Syrian, ibidem.
24. Ibidem.
25. Logos 3.
26. Logos 43.
27. Rule, prol.
28. Ladder 19, 4.
29. Centurie 1, 11.
30. Ladder 4, 92.

Seventh chapter

1. Instit. II.
2. 'Vigiliae privatae ... peculiare sacrificium' (Instit. II, 12, 3 and 13, 3).
3. Instit. III, 2.
4. Logos 30.
5. SC, 12.
6. Letter 74.
7. Apophthegms, Epiphanius, 3.
8. Dominus vobiscum, 6.
9. 'Licet remoti procul ab Ecclesia videamur per solitudinem corporum, in ea tamen praesentissimi semper assistimus per unitatis inviolabile sacramentum,' ibid., 10.
10. Ev. conc. expl. XIV, 24; cf. Matt. 18, 20.
11. Centurie, 7.
12. Adam Scot, De quadripertito exercitio cellae, 24.
13. De interiori domo, 5.
14. Grimlaïcus, Regula solitariorum, 32.
15. Adam Scot, ibid., 28.
16. William of S. Thierry, Golden Letter, II, 1.
17. De interiori domo, 82.
18. Barsanuphius and John, Letters 23 and 182.

19. Ladder 27.
20. Vita S. Mart., 26.
21. Logos 35, 174.
22. Apophthegms, Macarius, 19.
23. Instit. II, 10, 3.
24. Ladder, 28.
25. De instit. inclus., 18.
26. Centurie I, 89; I, 96; II, 4; II, 94.
27. In Cant. 15.
28. Golden Letter, I, 29.
29. Evagrius, de Oratione, 124.
30. Le Milieu Divin, III, 3, b.
31. Le milieu Mystique, in Writings in time of War.
32. In Matt. 55, 5.
33. In Gen. 42, 5.
34. Logos 21.
35. Apophthegms, Arsenius, 19.

The Lute-player
1. PG 147, 813s; taken over later on into the Philakalion.
2. John Climacus, Ladder, 28.